JESUS
AND THE
DAWN
OF
HOPE

Walking with Christ Through the Holy Week
to the Miraculous Easter Morning

DR. BRUCE L. HARTMAN

HIGH BRIDGE BOOKS
HOUSTON

CONTENTS

IT IS ALWAYS A GOOD MORNING!

THE SKY DARKENED, CASTING A SOMBER HUE OVER THE landscape; a profound sense of foreboding hung heavy in the air. The infamous hill of Calvary loomed ominously before the crowd that had gathered to witness the heartrending spectacle about to unfold. Crucifixion was an excruciatingly cruel form of punishment, reserved for the most heinous criminals and dissenters. But on this fateful day, it was not a criminal or a rebel who was to face the wooden cross; instead, it was a man whose life and teachings had and would touch countless souls.

Jesus of Nazareth, the man who had walked among the people with humility and compassion, now bore the weight of the world upon his bruised and bloodied shoulders. The events of the past hours had escalated swiftly, leading to this heart-wrenching conclusion. Betrayed by one of his own disciples, arrested unjustly, and subjected to a fraudulent trial, Jesus was now to be crucified alongside two criminals.

Upon reaching Calvary's summit, the soldiers roughly threw Jesus to the ground. His body, already weakened from the merciless beatings and the heavy burden of carrying the cross, struggled to find the strength to stand. As they positioned him on the cross, his gaze met the tearful eyes of some devoted followers who had braved the authorities to witness this tragic moment.

The crucifixion site was a haunting sight, with three crosses erected against the darkening sky. The criminal on the left side of Jesus cursed and spat, his heart consumed by bitterness and hatred. The criminal on the right was filled with compassion and regretful of the life he lived.

But in the midst of this cruelty, Jesus remained resolute, his eyes filled not with anger but with an unfathomable love and forgiveness.

While the soldiers hammered the nails through Jesus' outstretched hands and feet, and as each blow resounded, the anguished cries of onlookers pierced the air. Yet, in an astonishing act of compassion, Jesus uttered words that would echo through the annals of time: "Father, forgive them, for they know not what they do."

Despite the agony that coursed through his body, his thoughts were not of himself, but of those who sought to end his life. His willingness to forgive, even in the face of excruciating torment, showcased the depth of his divinity and the magnitude of his mission. This was a moment that transcended human understanding, a moment of ultimate sacrifice for the redemption of humankind.

In the hours that followed, the sun continued its descent, casting its dimming golden rays upon the hill of Calvary. The sky darkened, mirroring the grief that gripped the hearts of those who watched as Jesus hung between heaven and earth. In those moments of darkness, even nature seemed to mourn the injustice that had befallen a man of such purity and goodness.

Amidst the despair, Jesus spoke again, his voice barely a whisper, to the criminal on his right who had expressed remorse for his misdeeds. "Truly, I say to you, today you will be with me in paradise." Even in the throes of his own suffering, Jesus offered compassion and the promise of eternal life to a repentant soul.

As the final moments approached, Jesus cried out in a voice that carried both anguish and triumph, "It is finished." With those words, he proclaimed that his mission of love, reconciliation, and redemption had been fulfilled. And with a final breath, he surrendered his spirit to God.

The earth trembled, as if shaken by the weight of this extraordinary sacrifice. The veil of the temple tore in two, symbolizing the opening of a new covenant between God and humanity. Jesus' crucifixion was not the end but the beginning—a catalyst for a profound transformation that would touch the lives of billions.

The crucifixion of Jesus Christ remains a poignant reminder of the extent to which love can endure suffering and forgive transgressions. It stands as a testament to the triumph of compassion over cruelty and the eternal message that even in humanity's darkest hour, hope and redemption are possible.

And so, on that hill of Calvary, a chapter in human history was written—a chapter that continues to inspire, challenge, and move hearts with its unwavering message of love and redemption.

It Is Always a Good Morning!

While attending theological school, I enrolled in a Sunday worship course. Our professor, Dr. Heather Elkins, was a cherished mentor to many. Possessing a joyful spirit, she would become deeply earnest when discussing Jesus.

I held Dr. Elkins in high esteem for her candor and wonderfully rich insights. Her perspectives were always rooted in authenticity, shaped by her unique journey.

Years prior, she pursued theological education during an era when women were not fully accepted in ministerial roles. Despite her academic achievements, she wasn't granted any pastoral assignments. Undeterred, she returned to her hometown in West Virginia and established her own ministry at a truck stop.

In that diner's rear booth, Dr. Elkins provided counsel and comfort. She lent an attentive ear to truckers, locals, and other patrons, cultivating her pastoral skills in this unconventional setting. As the Methodist church gradually recognized the invaluable contributions of women, Dr. Elkins transitioned back into official pastoral roles, serving as both a minister and a college professor.

Her time as a "truck stop minister" had left an indelible mark. Engaging with people in moments of vulnerability at that diner had refined her listening skills and enhanced her empathy. Her unwavering commitment to Jesus guided her life, with the crucifixion's significance at its core.

One day, she greeted our class with a bright "Good morning!" We echoed back, but her subsequent question, "Why is it a good morning?" gave us pause. While we provided tentative answers, she enlightened us, emphasizing the importance of sensitivity when addressing congregations since not every member might be having a "good" day.

Her words resonated with a recent observation of mine: a lone, distraught woman in a church I had visited. Her grief was palpable and heart wrenching. I had wished to console her but couldn't locate her post-service. She was not having a good morning!

Dr. Elkins offered an alternative greeting, "It is always a good morning because Jesus rose." This statement encapsulated hope and the essence of Christian faith. The certainty of Jesus' resurrection remains an anchoring truth in my life, a beacon of hope and redemption even in the most turbulent of times.

In our challenging moments, we can find solace in the resurrection of Jesus. It is a testament to salvation, redemption, and eternal love.

Amidst daily distractions, we will always have and be able to cherish Jesus' sacrifice on that first Easter, a timeless act of love transcending all human struggles.

1

PALM SUNDAY

Nissan 10 (Sunday, March 29, AD 33)

JESUS SAT PATIENTLY ON A ROCK ON THE OUTSKIRTS OF Bethany. He had arrived late the previous day with the Twelve, having traveled through Jericho from a wilderness outpost in Samaria. As he sat, he mentally rehearsed what he needed to accomplish in the upcoming days. The commencement of his greatest mission would be today.

A few hours earlier, he had dispatched two of the Twelve into Jerusalem to fetch a young donkey, which he intended to ride into the city. As Jesus pondered the forthcoming week, he spotted the two men he had sent to Jerusalem in the distance, returning with the young donkey he had asked for. They had just left Jerusalem and were now headed back to Bethany, where Jesus and the Twelve were lodging.

The Twelve accompanying Jesus were known as the apostles. They were termed "apostles" because they were closest to Jesus, symbolizing the link between God's old covenant with the 12 tribes of Israel and the new covenant Jesus was introducing to humankind. Notably, the number 12 in the Bible represents the "perfection of governance."

It's common for people to confuse the terms "disciples" and "apostles." While all apostles were disciples, not all disciples were elevated to the status of apostles. Those referred to as "disciples" were either personally chosen by Jesus or sought to join his movement. For example, in Luke 10, Jesus dispatched 72 disciples to spread his teachings and perform healings. They were disciples, but not apostles. The apostles, numbering 12, journeyed with Jesus for three years and were his consistent and trusted companions.

Upon noticing the men, Jesus, placing his hands on his knees, gradually stood from the rock. Observing this, those with him shifted their gaze to Jesus. Through his eyes and a subtle nod, Jesus signaled it was time to depart.

Walking toward the two returning men, Jesus surveyed the hills encircling Jerusalem, taking in the budding hues of spring. After the bleak, rain-soaked winter, the world was rejuvenating. Jesus took a deep breath, comprehending it was now his time to ascend to the Holy City of Jerusalem to embark on his ultimate earthly mission. This Sunday morning marked the onset of a pivotal week—a week to confront humanity's foes: pride, greed, and fear—the very pillars of sin.

The path to meet the two men was predominantly uphill. Bethany, where Jesus and the Twelve were staying, lay on the southeastern slopes of the Mount of Olives. After their rendezvous, they would enjoy a brief, two-mile hike to enter Jerusalem.

The climate was a pleasant 70 degrees with a gentle breeze. The aroma of spring enveloped Jesus and the Twelve. The apostles, though silent, internally questioned the prudence of entering Jerusalem at this time. They were perplexed by Jesus' decision, aware of the imminent danger awaiting him in the city. Although they anticipated vast crowds of admiring locals and visiting pilgrims, they also recognized the presence of influential figures desiring to eliminate Jesus.

In recent times, wherever Jesus journeyed, he was greeted by adoring masses. Yet, in every locale, detractors sought to challenge and discredit him. While many viewed him as a beacon of hope, he was also perceived as a menace, particularly among the powerful in Jerusalem.

First-Century Conditions in Jerusalem

Jerusalem and its surrounding regions were divided between two groups: the haves and have-nots. The majority were born into the lower echelons, which often meant a life marked by persistent poverty, a daily battle to provide for oneself and one's family. This life was predominantly characterized by a state of want. Yet, Jesus offered hope to these masses. Conversely, he posed a threat to the powerful elites who exploited the common folk for their own gains.

For these elites, deceit and cunning were indispensable skills. Driven by an insatiable greed and a fervent desire to safeguard their riches, they prioritized self-preservation. Their lives revolved around their own interests, expecting to be served rather than to serve others.

In Jerusalem, those who wielded power comprised the civic and religious leadership: the Sanhedrin, the Pharisees, the scribes, and the Sadducees. They harbored a strong animosity towards Jesus. They recognized that Jesus could jeopardize their delicate ties with Rome, the local nobility, and the general populace. Over the past year, they had observed with increasing unease as Jesus captivated the hearts of many, undermining their long-established authority.

These leaders were well-acquainted with stories of Jesus' miraculous deeds, including resurrecting the dead, and the vast gatherings that awaited him in every town. Jesus was not just another fleeting sensation, unlike many who had come before him; he represented a genuine challenge.

Although they were well-informed about Jesus' actions, their greed and arrogance prevented them from recognizing him as a symbol of hope and redemption. Accepting Jesus for who he was would jeopardize their comfortable existence. Instead, they resolved to eliminate him.

The Twelve understood that this influential group was determined to remove Jesus, even if it meant resorting to murder. Silently, they pondered whether Jesus might be better off avoiding Jerusalem temporarily. Perhaps a return could be planned for a later date when the atmosphere was less charged.

Caiaphas, a Ruthless Leader

The most prominent leader in Jerusalem was the chief priest, Caiaphas. He had served in this capacity for an unusually lengthy period of 15 years.[1] He succeeded his father-in-law, Annas, after two other chief priests held the position briefly for two years. Annas himself had served as chief priest for nine years. Together, they had controlled the temple and Jerusalem for a combined 24 years. Annas had specifically chosen Caiaphas to succeed him and even arranged for Caiaphas to marry his daughter.

Caiaphas was a master manipulator. With persistent strategy, he established a powerful alliance with Annas, other religious leaders, the aristocracy, and the ruling Romans. He skillfully wielded fear and greed as tools, employing subtle threats or promises of money to get his way.

Caiaphas was astute in his maneuvers, capitalizing on timing and circumstance to extract power and wealth. Always calculating, he would wait patiently, observing the dynamics at play, even when others acted hastily. A ruthless despot, he was driven solely by his own greed. He viewed the world through his lens of manipulation and cunning, trusting no one and relentlessly striving for control.

As the chief priest, Caiaphas also presided over the Sanhedrin, a semi-political and religious body that Rome permitted to assist in governing Jerusalem. To Caiaphas, maintaining Rome's favor was paramount, with the Sanhedrin playing an essential role in this balancing act.

Caiaphas had adeptly managed the administrators Rome dispatched to oversee Judea. In fact, 15 years earlier, with Annas's assistance, he persuaded the then Roman prefect, Valerius Gratus, to endorse his appointment as the chief priest.[2]

The Romans, despite recognizing Caiaphas's lack of virtue, understood his capability to maintain order among the masses and elites. This ability made Jerusalem and Judea more manageable for the Roman Empire, requiring fewer military resources.

History of the Roman Rule of Jerusalem

For nearly 100 years, Jerusalem and its surrounding area were under the control of the Roman Empire. The Roman general Pompey conquered Jerusalem in 63 BC, ending the reign of the Hasmonean dynasty. By 37 BC, King Herod the Great emerged as a Roman client king and commenced his rule.[3] As Rome expanded its empire, it often appointed trusted quasi-monarchs from distant territories of non-Roman descent to assist in their governance; these rulers were termed "client kings."

King Herod was dubbed "the Great" not because of his character but for his architectural achievements. He elevated the stature of Jerusalem and Judea. Among his most significant feats was the extensive expansion of Jerusalem's temple. Once finished, it stood as a grand edifice, rivaling any structure in the Roman Empire.

However, Herod also had a sinister side. To successfully govern a segment of the Roman Empire, a Roman client king had to be unyieldingly ruthless. Otherwise, Rome's leadership would swiftly replace him. A cornerstone of Rome's imperial strategy was to quash rebellions decisively and brutally.

During this era, Rome's dominion was vast, spanning from present-day Great Britain to North Africa and from Syria to Spain. One out of every four people on Earth lived and died under Roman governance.[4] To manage such an expansive realm, Rome adopted a dual approach: it exerted brutal force in rebellious areas and appointed local leaders in more peaceful regions.

Herod's rule exemplified this strategy. In one infamous instance, he ordered the massacre of thousands of male infants in response to the birth of a boy the locals hailed as a king. This atrocity transpired around the onset of the first millennium, close to Jesus' birth.

Three magi from the East journeyed to Jerusalem, drawn by prophecies of a newborn destined to be the King of the Jews. They inquired, "Where is the one who has been born King of the Jews? We saw his star when it rose and have come to worship him" (Matt. 2:2).

Upon hearing this, Herod was both intrigued and alarmed. He sought to ascertain the validity of this potential threat to his and Rome's reigns in Judea. Summoning temple priests and learned scribes, he probed for information. During this session, one priest mentioned prophecies pinpointing Bethlehem as the child's birthplace. Another remarked on the similarity between recent events and ancient predictions. Still another told Herod the child's name was Jesus.

After the meeting, deep in thought, Herod concluded that he would employ the magi to locate the boy. When his guards located the magi, Herod warmly welcomed them, feigning joy and interest. He covertly gathered information, hoping to find and eliminate the infant Jesus, perceived as a potential rival.

As the magi departed, Herod requested they report back after locating the child, under the pretense of wishing to worship him. They assented, although they harbored suspicions regarding Herod's intent.

The magi eventually discovered Jesus in Bethlehem, guided by a star. Upon entering the barn where Mary cradled Jesus, they were filled with joy and offered gifts of gold, frankincense, and myrrh (Matt. 2:11-12).

Though initially intending to relay their findings to Herod, an angelic warning prompted them to return home by an alternative route.

Enraged by their evasion, Herod ordered the execution of all male infants under two in Bethlehem and neighboring regions.

Jesus evaded this fate due to an angelic intervention advising his family's flight to Egypt. Tragically, many others were not spared.

This heart-wrenching event is remembered as the Massacre of the Innocents. Numerous Christian sects commemorate these children, observing the day called Holy Innocents Day on either December 27th or 29th. While precise numbers remain elusive, it's believed that thousands of boys were slain.

In a twist of fate, not long after, Herod the Great met a painful end in Jericho, plagued by severe itching, chronic convulsions, and gangrene.[5] The historian Josephus labeled his affliction "Herod's Evil" and noted that Herod even contemplated suicide due to the agony.[6]

Following Herod's demise, Emperor Caesar Augustus endorsed Herod Antipas, Herod the Great's son, as the Roman ruler of Judea. Together, both Herods governed Judea for 75 years.

Historically, Roman provinces that remained compliant and fulfilled tax obligations enjoyed a semblance of autonomy. During this period, Jerusalem experienced relative tranquility, thanks largely to the shrewd and authoritative leadership of both Herods.

Political and Religious Leaders of Jerusalem

Jesus and the Twelve had arrived in Bethany the previous afternoon. With the sun dimming, Jesus gathered the Twelve around him. Sensing the weight of what was about to be shared, the Twelve drew closer, their faces etched with a mix of curiosity and concern.

Jesus began, "You have seen the religious leaders and the aristocrats of our time. They walk around in flowing robes, demanding respect, yet inside, many of them are like whitewashed tombs— clean on the outside but full of decay within." He paused, ensuring the gravity of his words sank in. "In their quest for power and position, many have lost sight of the very essence of our faith."

Peter, always eager, interjected, "But Rabbi, aren't they the chosen leaders of our people? Aren't they appointed to guide us in the ways of the Law?"

Jesus responded gently, "Peter, leadership is not about titles or positions. It's about humility, service, and love. While there are those among the leaders who are sincere, many more are more interested in their status and the praises of men. Remember how they challenge and test me."

John, with a hint of anger in his eyes, said, "Like Caiaphas. He claims to serve God, but he seems more interested in preserving his position than truly knowing God's heart."

Jesus nodded, "Caiaphas, as the high priest, is in a place of significant influence. Yet, he, like many others, feels threatened by the message we bring. They have built a system that benefits them, and anything that appears to disrupt this system becomes a threat. Caiaphas fears losing control, losing the favor of the Romans, and ultimately, his position."

James then questioned, "But why can't they see, Lord? Why can't they understand that you're fulfilling the very prophecies they've studied for years?"

With a sigh, Jesus replied, "It's a matter of the heart, James. True understanding doesn't just come from knowledge. It comes from a heart open to God's spirit. The scriptures, the prophecies—they all point towards love, redemption, and grace. But when one's heart is hardened by pride, power, or the desire for control, it becomes difficult to see and accept the truth."

Andrew pondered aloud, "So, what do we do, Rabbi? How do we approach these leaders?"

Jesus, looking intently at each of the apostles, responded, "Continue to speak the truth in love. Be wise as serpents but innocent as doves. Not all will accept the message, but some will have ears to hear. And remember, even in the face of opposition, My Father's plan will prevail. In the end, even Caiaphas, in his actions, will unknowingly play a part in bringing it to fruition."

Jesus went on to explain their mission for the everyday person in Jerusalem by saying, "Jerusalem is not just a city of priests and rulers; it's also home to countless souls, many of whom live lives burdened by daily struggles and challenges."

He continued, "Many of the people there live under the weight of Roman occupation, facing heavy taxation and limited freedoms. Their daily lives revolve around work, often demanding and back-breaking, just to earn enough for their family's sustenance.

The rich and the Temple elite may walk the streets in grandeur, but the average person, the heart of this city, grapples with the stark realities of poverty, disease, and constant uncertainty. They seek hope, a respite from their struggles, and the promise of something greater."

Leaning in closer, Jesus said with emphasis, "It's for these very souls we bring the message of God. They need to know that their worth isn't determined by their social status or wealth, but by the love of our father in heaven. While their earthly burdens are real and pressing, the hope and love we share offer a peace that transcends their immediate circumstances. Remember always to approach them with compassion and understanding, for in serving them, we serve the father."

The Twelve sat in thoughtful silence, absorbing the depth and implications of Jesus' words. They were slowly beginning to grasp the challenge and promise of their mission, a mission that would transform not just Jerusalem but the entire world.

Raising Lazarus—The Turning Point

Of particular concern for Caiaphas and the Sanhedrin was Jesus raising a local man from the dead three months earlier. This incident had caused many to cross over from just wondering about Jesus to believing he was their answer—perhaps the long-awaited Messiah.

Jesus had been on the eastern side of the Jordan River, near where John the Baptist had baptized him, after narrowly escaping being stoned in Jerusalem. During his visit in the Holy city he had stated,

> Do not believe me unless I do the works of my Father.
> But if I do them, even though you do not believe me,

believe the works, that you may know and understand
that the Father is in me, and I in the Father. (Jn. 10:37–38)

After this statement caused an uproar, Jesus and the Twelve
went east to the other side of the Jordan River to avoid further conflict.

While Jesus was on the eastern shore of the Jordan, two sisters,
Martha and Mary, who lived in Bethany, faced a crisis. Their
brother, Lazarus, had fallen ill and was on the brink of death. Martha
and Mary were early believers in Jesus as the Messiah, particularly
since Jesus had healed their father from the debilitating effects of
leprosy. In gratitude, the sisters, along with Lazarus and their father,
became devoted followers of Jesus. Due to their deep faith, Jesus had
developed a special bond with the family. Thus, when Lazarus became critically ill, they immediately sent word to Jesus, seeking his
help.

When Jesus received word of Lazarus's illness, he said, "This
sickness will not end in death. No, it is for God's glory so that God's
Son may be glorified through it" (Jn. 11:4). Remarkably, Jesus didn't
go to them immediately; he waited two days. Then, on the third day,
he told the Twelve,

> "Let's go back to Judea."
> "But Rabbi," they said, "a short while ago the Jews
> there tried to stone you, and yet you are going back?"
> Jesus replied, "Are there not twelve hours of day-
> light? Anyone who walks in the daytime will not stum-
> ble, for they see by this world's light. It is when a person
> walks at night that they stumble, for they have no light."
> (Jn. 11:7–10)

After this, Jesus told them Lazarus had only fallen asleep. But
still fearful, the Twelve said, "Lord, if he sleeps, he will get better"
(Jn. 11:13). But the Twelve still didn't understand.

Then Jesus became franker and said, "Lazarus is dead, and for your sake I am glad I was not there, so that you may believe. But let us go to him" (Jn. 11:14–15). Jesus had a plan. While it included saving a close friend, it also included showing many others the glory of God.

The Twelve did not want to go anywhere near Jerusalem, knowing Jesus was despised by Caiaphas and the other leaders. Getting this close to Jerusalem threatened both Jesus' life and their own, so they appealed to Jesus not to go.

However, the always loyal and pragmatic Thomas said to the other 11, "Let us also go, that we may die with him" (Jn. 11:16). Thomas knew that by going to help Lazarus, the whole band of apostles might be killed. Despite the risk, he was driven by his strict loyalty to Jesus. Interestingly, Thomas, throughout the centuries, has been called *the doubting Thomas,* but here we find a loyal Thomas, willing to die with and for Jesus.

In contemporary times, many have mistaken Thomas's pragmatism for doubt. As evidenced by his willingness to go with Jesus, we can see that nothing could be further from the truth. Though pragmatic, his loyalty to Jesus and his search for truth would become very evident during the following months.

As they approached Bethany, Martha met them and said to Jesus,

> "If you had been here, my brother would not have died. But I know that even now God will give you whatever you ask."
>
> Jesus said to her, "Your brother will rise again."
>
> Martha answered, "I know he will rise again in the resurrection at the last day."
>
> Jesus said to her, "I am the resurrection and the life. The one who believes in me will live, even though they die; and whoever lives by believing in me will never die. Do you believe this?"

"Yes, Lord," she replied, "I believe that you are the Messiah, the Son of God, who is to come into the world." (Jn. 11:21–27)

Martha's faith in Jesus was very evident; her faith exceeded that of many, including the Twelve who had been traveling with Jesus.

Martha went back to Mary and told her Jesus was coming. Ecstatic, Mary and many friends immediately went to the outskirts of Bethany to meet Jesus. The many friends who were with Mary to comfort her because of her brother's death followed her.

As she approached Jesus, he could see she was crying. He also saw the many friends with her, and, in his full humanity, he became deeply moved and troubled. He said:

Where have you laid him?
The crowd replied, "Come and see, Lord." (Jn. 11:33; 34)

Jesus, seeing the outpouring of grief, in his humanness, began to weep as well.

Many in the crowd exclaimed, "See how he loved him."

But some cynically asked, "Could not he who opened the eyes of the blind man have kept this man from dying?" (Jn. 11:36-37).

Those who were cynical were referring to an earlier incident in which Jesus had healed a beggar who had been blind since birth. This event had caused an uproar among the Pharisees because Jesus had healed the man on the Sabbath. Instead of being thankful or amazed that Jesus had performed this feat, they criticized him.

In turn, their uproar had only served to make the Pharisees look silly to those who had heard of or witnessed the miraculous event.

As he usually did, Jesus ignored the cynical and doubters, continuing toward Lazarus's burial tomb. Upon his arrival, Jesus asked that the stone be removed. Martha, worried about the potential bad odor after the body had lain there for several days, warned Jesus against removing the stone. However, Jesus looked at Martha and said, "Did I not tell you that if you believe, you will see the glory of God?" (Jn. 11:40). Those near the tomb then removed the stone.

Looking around at the crowd, Jesus knew many in the crowd would become witnesses of his upcoming actions. Raising his head with his arms outstretched, he looked up to the sky and said,

> Father, I thank you that you have heard me. I knew that you always hear me, but I say this for the benefit of the people standing here, that they may believe that you sent me. (Jn. 11:41–42)

In this statement, notice Jesus uses the word "knew" instead of the more appropriate word "know." This subtle difference is an expression of the closeness between God and Jesus and is not a linguistic error.

After saying this, Jesus loudly commanded Lazarus to "come forth." Lazarus emerged from the tomb, wrapped in strips of linen with cloth on his face. Jesus asked those nearby to unbind him and dress him.

Many of the crowd who had come to comfort Martha and Mary saw this and were amazed. Weeping, some even fell to their knees and looked up to the sky and thanked God. Most who were present now believed Jesus was more than a great healer; he was their Savior.

But some, hoping to gain favor, went to the leaders in Jerusalem and told them what had happened.

Upon hearing about this event, Caiaphas quickly convened a meeting of the Sanhedrin to discuss the reports surrounding Jesus and the resurrection of Lazarus. Caiaphas requested a detailed account of Lazarus being raised from the dead. Those who had gathered information from the attendees relayed what they had learned. By and large, the accounts from these individuals were consistent with the testimonies of eyewitnesses. The more Caiaphas and the Sanhedrin heard, the more alarmed they became.

Many who witnessed the event came to believe that Jesus was sent by God, a belief that deeply concerned Caiaphas and the other leaders. Distraught and fearful, some members of the Sanhedrin posed a question to Caiaphas, "What are we accomplishing? Here is this man performing many miracles. If we allow him to continue in this way, everyone will believe in him. The Romans will then intervene, seizing both our temple and our nation" (Jn. 11:47–48).

The gravity of both scenarios was becoming increasingly evident. Undoubtedly, Jesus was presenting a novel way of life to the common people, one that wasn't predicated on fear. The Romans recognized that the Sanhedrin and the priests held sway over the masses, which facilitated their governance. Jesus' burgeoning influence among the locals jeopardized this delicate balance.

Caiaphas realized that it was time to address the threat of Jesus. He also understood the Sanhedrin needed to not act rashly. Jesus' removal would have to be executed with care and tact to avoid inciting public unrest. It would be challenging but achievable with skillful action. They needed to remain calm as they moved against Jesus.

News of this meeting reached Jesus through those who had overheard the discussions and the subsequent decisions. Knowing it wasn't yet his time to confront the leaders of Jerusalem, he withdrew from the public eye, retreating to the wilderness and the ancient tribal community of Ephraim.

A millennium earlier, the people of Ephraim had merged with the people of Manasseh, forming one of the original 12 tribes of Israel. The tribes had been led to the promised land under God's guidance through Moses and Joshua.

After enduring centuries under erratic rulers, the original 12 tribes of Israel fragmented. Ten of them, including Ephraim, constituted the kingdom of Israel. The remaining two, Judah and Benjamin, established the kingdom of Judah, with Jerusalem as its heart.

Both kingdoms eventually fell to foreign dominions. The Assyrians overtook the kingdom of Israel, leading to the ten tribes' dissolution. In Jesus' era, the territory of these tribes was referred to as

Samaria. Judah, on the other hand, was conquered by the Babylonians around 600 BC. Despite efforts, Judah never fully regained its autonomy, falling subsequently to the likes of Alexander the Great. By the first century BC, Rome had dominion over both Judah and Samaria.

Tensions mounted between Judah and Samaria over the years. Judeans perceived the Samaritans as lesser kin. The Assyrian occupation saw many from the ten tribes intermarrying with Assyrians and neighboring tribes. This blending of lineages produced a mixed population, perceived by the Judeans as a dilution of purity, relegating the Samaritans to a lower status.

In Jesus' compassionate approach, no group was considered lesser—everyone was deserving of God's love. Consequently, Jesus often ministered in Samaria, treating its inhabitants with dignity and respect. One of his most renowned parables is "The Good Samaritan," which he shared after a scribe asked, "Who is my neighbor?" (Lk. 10:29). Through this tale, Jesus emphasized that every individual was deserving of God's affection.

On another occasion, as depicted in John 4, Jesus encountered a Samaritan woman at a well. During this interaction, Jesus revealed his identity as the Messiah, leading the woman to advocate for him among her people. Many Samaritans were among the first to acknowledge Jesus as the Son of God and the Messiah. To Jesus, the Samaritans were souls worth saving. His message was clear: devotion to God wasn't a matter of nationality, race, or gender, but it hinged on one's heart and regard for fellow humans.

Retreating to Ephraim in Samaria was a strategic move for Jesus as it was less frequented by those from Judah or Jerusalem. This allowed him a safe haven, buying time until the opportune moment to return to Jerusalem.

Lazarus's resurrection had a dual effect: many were convinced Jesus was the Messiah, which strengthened Caiaphas's resolve to eliminate him. Although Caiaphas had considered arresting Jesus before the Lazarus incident, he now felt the urgency to act.

The atmosphere set the stage for a strategic game of cat-and-mouse between Jesus and Caiaphas in the imminent future.

Jesus Enters Jerusalem on Palm Sunday

Jesus stayed in Ephraim, waiting for the right time. A few months later, just before the holy week of Passover, Jesus and the Twelve arrived in Bethany near Jerusalem. While the Twelve didn't understand why, Jesus' goal was to celebrate Passover in Jerusalem. Jesus knew hundreds of thousands of Jews from neighboring areas would be descending upon the Holy City. During the Passover week, Jesus would have a large audience, enabling him to teach and be shielded from the authorities because of their presence.

Regardless of the danger, Jesus knew his mission and was followed back to Jerusalem by a reluctant and astonished group of 12 apostles. First, they had to go to Bethany, where they would stay. The trek to Bethany was a three-days' hike, or 40 miles, from where they were. [7]

As they walked to Bethany from Ephraim, Jesus explained himself to the Twelve by saying,

> We are going up to Jerusalem, and the Son of Man will be delivered over to the chief priests and the teachers of the law. They will condemn him to death and will hand him over to the Gentiles, who will mock him and spit on him, flog him and kill him. Three days later he will rise. (Mk. 10:33–34)

Upon hearing Jesus say this, the Twelve were bewildered. Why would Jesus visit a place where he thought he would be killed? Why would he subject himself to known terror? At this point, the Twelve were utterly confused. Even though they had spent many days and hours with Jesus, they still underestimated Jesus' divinity, seeing Jesus through their own eyes and logic. What Jesus was doing and said about this trip defied human logic.

Early in the morning, after their arrival in Bethany, Jesus sent two of the Twelve into Jerusalem to retrieve a young donkey. Jesus told them,

> Go to the village ahead of you, and just as you enter it, you will find a colt tied there, which no one has ever ridden. Untie it and bring it here. If anyone asks you, "Why are you doing this?" say, "The Lord needs it and will send it back here shortly." (Mk. 11:2–3)

When the two men entered Jerusalem an hour or so later, at the door to the Golden Gate stood a colt, just as Jesus had said. The colt was a young male donkey. Over the years, there has been some confusion regarding whether Jesus rode in on a donkey or a colt. Because in this case they are both one and the same, the answer is *yes*.

The two who had been sent began untying the donkey colt to take it to Jesus, but curious onlookers asked them what they were doing. The two men replied, "Jesus needs the colt; he will be riding it into Jerusalem today." So, upon hearing it was for Jesus, the now enthusiastic onlookers helped the two untie the colt. Then, the two men left the city again through the Golden Gate and returned to Bethany.

There were eight gates into the Holy City of Jerusalem. The Golden Gate, where the colt stood, is called today the Gate of Mercy and has been closed for centuries. Prior to Jesus' arrival, ancient Jewish tradition believed that the Messiah would enter through the Golden Gate from the Mount of Olives,[8] as he would on this day.

For Jesus, the Golden Gate was the quickest way to enter the city from Bethany. It also provided the easiest access to the temple and its sprawling courtyards.

As the two men with the colt headed back down to Bethany, they spotted Jesus and quickened their pace toward him. When they met Jesus, they put a cloak on the donkey colt. Jesus thanked them and mounted the young animal to begin his journey into Jerusalem. The two-mile ride into Jerusalem would take him about an hour.

Those in Jerusalem who had helped untie the donkey told many that Jesus was coming into Jerusalem. Upon hearing this, many in the city began to assemble around the Golden Gate and line the path that led into Jerusalem. *Jesus was coming!*

During the past year of his earthly ministry, Jesus had gotten accustomed to having large crowds appear when people knew he was coming to any town. Lately, when he'd gone to cities like Capernaum or when people knew he would be by a lake, thousands would show up. The masses loved him and believed he was the Messiah who would lead them out of their lives of desperation.

There had been many other prophets who had proclaimed they were the Messiah, but most believed Jesus was different. Those other prophets had only offered false hope and empty promises. The masses saw right through those magicians and watched as they tried to take advantage of the people's desire to be rid of a life with no freedom and scant resources.

While the Jews were a destitute people and had been that way for centuries, they knew who was real and who wasn't. They saw Jesus didn't want money for his miracles or fame for his exploits. He wanted to be their servant and help them in their lives.

Jesus entered the outskirts of the city where ramshackle shacks lined his route. To his right and down the hill was a field of poppy flowers, bright red from the recent winter rains. It was springtime, and all around the hills were beginning to glow with vibrant colors. In front of Jesus, people lined the path.

As he continued his climb up from the valley and beyond the outskirts of the city, more people started to appear on both his right and his left. Up ahead of him, the crowd grew even bigger, and he could see people jostling, trying to get the best view. This was an excited throng, waiting and anticipating his triumphant entry.

In ancient times, when kings would enter a town, they would ride in as mighty warriors on a majestic horse, which was a symbol of their power. Yet Jesus was riding in on a young donkey; this was a symbol he desired peace. In his humility, he had chosen the least of all livestock. It was a simple message of humbleness for those lining the road.

Spontaneously, some laid their cloaks down on the road, while others waved palm fronds in his path. Soon, the way in front of Jesus was filled with cloaks and people waving palm branches. As he passed, some in the crowd went ahead of him while others followed behind. The higher he climbed toward Jerusalem, the bigger the crowds grew. He was surrounded by a hopeful gathering—hopeful Jesus was their answer to a life of fear.

Then, from all around, the voices shouted:

> Hosanna!
> Blessed is he who comes in the name of the Lord!
> Blessed is the coming kingdom of our father, David!
> Hosanna in the highest heaven! (Mk. 11:10)

The procession continued until Jesus approached the Golden Gate. Upon reaching it, he gracefully dismounted, acknowledging the multitude with a glance and a gesture. He then moved forward, threading his way through the throng of onlookers.

The grandeur of Jerusalem's temple and its expansive courtyards stretched before him. The masses, having heard tales of his deeds, pressed closer, eager to glimpse the revered figure. Many voices called out while other people were moved to tears of joy.

Venturing further into the temple precincts, Jesus paused, surveying his surroundings before directing his steps to the Courtyard of the Gentiles. The scene that met his gaze was jarring. Merchants and money changers had set up shop, peddling livestock and offering currency exchange, especially for the imminent Passover meal. These commercial endeavors, Jesus realized, often exploited the devout. The day was waning, and time was not on his side, so he resolved to address this desecration of his Father's house tomorrow.

The crowd, having witnessed or heard of Jesus' miraculous acts, was expectant. Tales of him resurrecting Lazarus and banishing dark spirits were widespread. Many, now witnessing him firsthand, recognized the greatness of his teachings. There was a shared sentiment: in Jesus, they saw hope and the possibility of liberation from their hardships.

From atop the city's fortifications, Caiaphas and other religious elites observed Jesus' entrance. The sight of Jesus and the palpable fervor of the crowd, made Caiaphas uneasy. Jesus' timing, arriving in Jerusalem during the sacred Passover, was strategic, making any clandestine action against him risky amidst such numerous witnesses.

Jesus had started turning the wheels of destiny.

2

TURNING OVER THE TABLES

Nissan 11 (Monday, March 30, AD 33)

ON THE MONDAY MORNING OF PASSOVER WEEK, JESUS awoke with determination. He was deeply affected by what he had observed in the temple the previous day and was eager to return to Jerusalem. Today, he was singularly focused on addressing the inappropriate activities occurring in the temple.

The night before, he had sought solace in the Garden of Gethsemane, close to where he and the Twelve were staying. Entering the garden, he passed by two olive trees at its boundary. Ahead, in the dimly lit grove, he spotted a secluded area shielded by a stone outcrop. Reaching the spot, he sat, the smooth stone surface providing support for his back. The stone felt pleasantly cool. Closing his eyes, he sought silence and stillness, eventually achieving a state of peaceful meditation. In this serene moment, he aligned his thoughts and felt renewed strength from God. Sleep eventually overcame him, and he rested there until dawn.

As the sun began to illuminate the garden, Jesus stood up, collecting his thoughts and preparing for the day ahead. He was aware that while the majority had enthusiastically welcomed his entry into Jerusalem the previous day, the leadership was deeply unsettled.

His strategy of reentering Jerusalem during the protective ambiance of Passover had been effective. The vast crowds of devoted pilgrims and locals had shielded him, allowing his ministry to continue.

Fully aware that Caiaphas and other Jerusalem leaders were keen on eliminating him, Jesus recalled the upheaval caused by his resurrection of Lazarus some months earlier. Given the crowd's fervent support the prior day, Caiaphas had grown more anxious, realizing that Jesus was more formidable than he had initially estimated—surpassing all those who had previously claimed to be the awaited Messiah.

Today, Jesus was poised to rectify injustices and further his teachings. It would also be a day of challenging Caiaphas, potentially pushing him to make a rash decision. Beneath the splendor of Jesus' entry into Jerusalem, a battle of strategy and wit unfolded. While Caiaphas sought to capture and execute Jesus, Jesus was on an unfinished mission, needing more time. Up to this point, Jesus held the upper hand.

This day was significant for Jesus. He intended to challenge one of the primary sources of power and income for Caiaphas and the temple leaders. It was also an opportunity to advocate for the many pilgrims and locals in Jerusalem who were being exploited during the sacred Passover period—a time meant for reflection on how God, through Moses, had liberated the Israelites from Egyptian captivity. It wasn't about commerce.

It wasn't anger driving Jesus; indeed, anger wasn't an emotion he harbored. In his Sermon on the Mount, he had warned against the dangers of anger, equating it to a disruptive mental state akin to sin. Rather, he was profoundly dismayed by the desecration he witnessed in the temple. Addressing the temple's corruption would demand bold action. Today was yet another chance to guide the faithful and reemphasize the holiness of God.

The Fig Tree

After Jesus gathered the Twelve, they began their journey from Bethany to Jerusalem on empty stomachs. The early spring sun cast a warm glow, making their uphill trek to Jerusalem a pleasant walk.

Along the way, a fig tree, unusually lush for this time of the year, caught Jesus' eye. Typically, fig trees would just be sprouting leaves in this season. This particular tree, however, was bursting with greenery, hinting at the possibility of ripe fruit. The sight instilled hope among the Twelve that they might find something to satisfy their hunger.

But upon closer inspection, despite the thick foliage, the tree bore no figs, not even the early signs of them. Disappointed by the barrenness, Jesus declared, "May no one eat fruit from you again" (Mk. 11:14).

In a way, the fig tree's false promise of fruit mirrored what Jesus had observed in the temple the day before. From a distance, both offered a symbol of nourishment or sacredness, but upon closer look, both were empty. This symbolic link between fig trees and faithfulness has ancient roots. For instance, in Jeremiah 8:13, God likens the unfaithful to fruitless fig trees: "There will be no figs on the tree, and their leaves will wither. What I have given them will be taken from them."

Jesus turned to the twelve and said, "This fig tree will serve as a stark reminder of the repercussions of misusing God's gifts."

The encounter with the fig tree was more than just a chance event.

Entering the Courtyard of the Gentiles

The group continued up the hill to Jerusalem on a similar path to the one they had walked the day before. On this day, they would arrive unannounced in the town; there would be no crowds awaiting Jesus' arrival.

When the group arrived in Jerusalem, they entered through the Golden Gate. For Jesus, the Golden Gate provided easy access to the Courtyard of the Gentiles, where merchants would be selling their livestock and changing money.

Jesus strode through the gate, his steps quick and determined. His face was resolute and stern, reflecting a clear purpose. Troubled by what he had seen late the previous afternoon in the temple's Courtyard of the Gentiles, Jesus was on a mission.

He took a quick left, turning away from the Women's Courtyard near the temple. Jesus then proceeded along Solomon's Colonnade, which lined the east side of the temple. As he and the Twelve moved south, they saw the temple building to their right. Shortly after passing the main temple building, the Courtyard of the Gentiles came into view.

The Courtyard of the Gentiles was not part of the original temple but rather an addition. Along with other improvements, it had been initiated by Herod the Great in 19 BC. The courtyard served two specific purposes. First, it was a place where visitors, both Jewish and Gentile, could view the temple, much like modern-day tourists.

Second, it served as a market where people could buy and sell livestock or exchange money. During this week, the livestock purchased would either have been used for temple sacrifice or for the Passover meal. Money was also exchanged so visitors could make their temple donations.[9]

Jesus and the Twelve turned right toward the courtyard, walking under the covered Solomon's Colonnade. Along the colonnade, large groups of people were milling around. On this morning, the entire temple area was alive with pilgrims who had descended on Jerusalem to prepare for the Passover feast. If you stood under the colonnade and looked up, you would see the intricate red and gray squares that lined its ceiling. This was symbolic of the great detail and artistry that had been put into building this magnificent temple compound.

As they descended the steps of the colonnade, they got a firsthand look at the courtyard area and the many in the marketplace who were selling or buying. The courtyard was the only place in the temple complex non-Jewish people could access. Gentiles proceeding further into the sacred areas of the temple could be punished by death.[10]

Because of the courtyard's proximity to the temple, it was the best place for the merchants to sell their livestock and exchange money. The massive courtyard was 900 feet in length and 400 feet wide, equal to 9 acres.[11]

On this day, the courtyard was filled with tables, livestock, merchants, and pilgrims, with the buzz of men bartering very loud and present. Close to 300,000 people had descended on the city during this critical and sacred period. Throngs of people were buying and selling in the Courtyard of the Gentiles.

In the first century in Jerusalem, there were three pilgrimage festivals; one was in the fall, and two were in the spring. The biggest holiday of all, which brought pilgrims from all around, was the celebration of Passover.[12]

These pilgrimages were to celebrate Pesach (Passover), Shavuot (Festival of Weeks), and Sukkot (Harvest Festival). On this day, most people were there to celebrate Passover, which was a time to remember the great exodus from Egypt to escape pharaoh and the start of the 12 tribes' long journey to the promised land.

Jesus looked across the courtyard and then looked left. He watched merchants selling pigeons and livestock and saw money-changers sitting at their tables. Around the tables and booths were travelers bartering with merchants.

Further to Jesus' right, he saw some tables that went beyond the boundaries of the courtyard and extended into the sacred areas. Despite the prohibition of going into these areas, this was a common practice when the crowds were too large and the merchants needed more room. Seeing the merchants' tables expand into the sacred area, Jesus' frown deepened.

By the time Jesus arrived, there was already a large crowd of people buying their temple sacrifices. Whenever there was a major holiday, those visiting Jerusalem would visit the temple and make an animal sacrifice. These sacrifices were considered part of maintaining a right relationship with God.

During these holiday periods, people would often have to travel up to a thousand miles to get to Jerusalem, making it impractical to bring a suitable sacrificial animal with them. Bringing livestock with them had many hurdles. The first was that traveling many miles risked injury to the animal. The second was that the animal would have to be inspected by the priests and found to be unblemished.

With regard to the inspections, most knew no matter how pristine the condition of the animal, the corrupt priests would often find some reason to deny the animal as suitable for sacrifice. This would force the person to use one of the temple's vendors to purchase their sacrificial animal.

Many knew this was a rigged game, but, still, to satisfy both their desire to please God and the requirement to provide a sacrifice, they bought from the merchants.[13] While they knew they were being taken advantage of, it was the most practical method of complying with scripture and tradition.

The pilgrims would buy the animal at one of the booths or tables in this courtyard. Then the animal would be given to one of the priests in the temple for inspection and slaughter.

On Sunday, the previous day, Jesus had observed those buying the sacrificial lamb for the upcoming Passover celebration. This was a purchase to meet a different need: this lamb was for the Passover dinner. Some years, over 100,000 lambs were sold.[14]

As required by the Torah, the lamb to be sacrificed for the Passover supper had to be bought four days early to ensure its purity. The 10th day of Nissan was the traditional day to buy the lamb, and in the year AD 33, that day fell on a Sunday.

But this day, Monday, the 11th day of Nissan, was different; pilgrims were purchasing animals to make their temple sacrifice. If you were poor or a widow and couldn't afford an ox or a sheep, you would buy a pair of birds, likely pigeons.

As had been done the day before during the sale of Passover lambs, the animals used for the temple sacrifice were sold far above their market price.[15] Jesus was especially shocked to see the merchants overcharging the destitute and widows—an even more sullied act of greed.

Also, as part of this visit to the temple, it was customary to give a half-shekel for temple maintenance. During this time in the Middle East, the Roman denarius was the coin commonly used for everyday transactions.[16] As such, most of those visiting the temple only had denarii, which had to be converted to the sacred shekel.

The temple priest could only accept the shekel and not the denarius. The denarius bore an image of the emperor, Caesar Augustus, who was considered by Romans to be a god. Because of this image, the temple priests had declared the denarii impure and unacceptable for a sacrificial offering, forcing people to buy the half-shekel from the moneychangers. And they used rigged scales when exchanging the denarii, which provided another source of income.

A percentage of the merchants' and moneychangers' profits had to be given to the chief priest, Caiaphas. These required payments grew each year and made it harder for the merchants to make any money. In turn, under pressure to make a profit and satisfy Caiaphas, the merchants and moneychangers overcharged for the livestock, pigeons, and the conversion of the denarii into the shekel.

Caiaphas became very skilled at knowing how to make money off the merchants and demanded more and more from them each year. He knew their breaking point, and each year, he pushed the merchants to this point.

Caiaphas even organized the selling of the sacrificed livestock after their slaughter. The slaughtered remains of the sacrificed livestock were sold in the meat markets surrounding the temple. Essentially, Caiaphas had established an efficient money-making scheme from the pasture to the meat market. At every one of these unholy transactions, profits were skimmed.

Today was the day to act and make the temple a holy place again. Jesus was going to defend his father's house.

It wasn't that Jesus was upset by economic activity. In his youth, Jesus and his earthly dad, Joseph, had made furniture to sell. What Jesus saw in the temple wasn't hard work but rather scheming in the name of God to gain money without effort. Greed drove the temple leaders who used inappropriate power to earn money.

When Jesus arrived in the Courtyard of the Gentiles, he surveyed the scene to decide what to do next. He then gathered up some of the whips from nearby livestock booths. Next, Jesus called his disciples together, giving each of them a whip and telling them, "Follow my lead."

Purposefully, Jesus walked to the closest booth, flipped over the table, and used his whip to drive away the livestock. Upon seeing this, the Twelve did the same to the other tables and booths. Then, some in the crowd joined in as well. The scene became quite chaotic as Jesus, the Twelve, and people from the crowd flipped over tables—livestock were driven out of their pens, pigeons were released, and coins spilled out on the floor.

The vendors raised their voices and yelled for Jesus and everyone to stop. Shoppers were left stunned and unsure of what to do.

On it went with tables being quickly turned over. At first, it was just a few, but soon, there was a sea of flipped tables. Looking across the Courtyard of the Gentiles, the scene had the appearance of rippling, as one table after another was tipped over. The mayhem started with Jesus and spread quickly throughout the courtyard.

Everyone else who was present was frozen with disbelief. The priests and merchants had been caught off balance mentally; they stood absorbing the scene and were unprepared to act. When Jesus was done, the Courtyard of the Gentiles, which once had tables and booths lined up in an orderly fashion, was a scene of chaos with loose livestock roaming the courtyard area and the wings of birds flapping. Money collectors fell to their knees frantically scouring the ground to pick up the loose coins. Jesus had put an end to the charade.

"My House," Jesus' Temple

Then Jesus went and stood on the stairs leading down to the courtyard and exclaimed, "My house will be called a house of prayer for all nations. But you have made it a den of robbers" (Mk. 11:17). Next, Jesus told the Twelve to spread out and not let anyone carry or take anything out of the courtyard.

It is interesting that Jesus refers to the temple as "my house" in the Gospel of Mark. In two other gospels, Matthew and Luke, Jesus also refers to the temple as "my house." However, in the Gospel of John, Jesus refers to the temple as "my Father's house." The question for the reader could be, Is it Jesus' house or God's house? Both statements are accurate and not contradictory. To better understand why, let's look at John 1:1.

John 1:1 says, "In the beginning was the Word, and the Word was with God, and the Word was God." Through literary analysis of Greek and the author's intent, we discover the word "Word" is a reference to Jesus. In other words, we can rewrite the verse to say, "In the beginning was Jesus, and Jesus was with God, and Jesus was God." Rereading the verse this way helps us better understand who Jesus was and is.

Jesus is with God and is God—he existed from the beginning. Jesus is both a separate entity and part of the Godhead and most certainly divine. Similarly, the Holy Spirit is part of the Godhead and is God. This wonderful mystery is called the Holy Trinity.

The Holy Trinity is defined as one God, coexisting equally in three divine persons: God the Father, God the Son, and God the Holy Spirit. Understanding the Holy Trinity helps us resolve and understand Jesus' reference to "my house." It is Jesus' house, and it is also his father's house. This apparent contradiction is actually a clue to the Holy Trinity.

The Holy Trinity is not specifically spelled out in the four gospels, but there are many clues. It was not until 325 A.D. that it was fully discussed at a meeting in Nicaea. Out of this council meeting, the Nicene Creed was created to explain the Holy Trinity.

The temple, or Jesus' house in Jerusalem, had deep connections that dated back more than 1,000 years to Moses. During the exodus from Egypt, Moses spent 40 days on Mount Sinai and was given the Ten Commandments by God. Following God's direction, Moses placed them in an ark, which is known as the Ark of the Covenant or the Ark of God and was considered the most sacred relic of the Israelites.

The ark went with the Israelites on their 40-year journey to the promised land. At night, the ark was stored in an elaborate tent compound called the Tent of Meeting. In effect, the ark and the tent were the first temple.

When the Israelites crossed the Jordan River into the promised land, the Ark of the Covenant went in front of them and miraculously parted the Jordan River, which was at flood stage. God had told Joshua to have the priests carry the ark out into the raging waters of the river. And when they did, the river parted and provided the Israelites a dry path across the Jordan River, into the promised land.

After crossing the Jordan, the ark was kept in a town called Shiloh for many years.[17] Shiloh today is a popular archaeological site in Palestine and is called Khirbet Seilun.

Later, the Philistines captured the ark from the Israelites, only to become plagued by misfortune. In its final placement by the Philistines, the ark caused the people of the ancient Philistine city Ashdod to develop painful tumors. Alarmed and connecting their misfortunes to having stolen the ark, the Philistines returned the ark to the Israelites.

When David became king, he made plans to build a temple to house the ark. David was uncomfortable living in a grand palace while the ark was in a tent, but his desire for the ark to have a permanent home was refused by God. The word of God came to David saying, "You have shed much blood and have fought many wars. You are not to build a house for my name, because you have shed much blood on the earth in my sight" (1 Chr. 22:8). Instead, his son

Solomon received God's permission to use his father's plans and build the First Temple.

An interesting side note is the temple stood on the same place Abraham had almost sacrificed Isaac.[18] God had told Abraham to sacrifice his son Isaac. Upon seeing Abraham's obedience, God intervened and provided a ram to be sacrificed instead.

Isaac later had a son named Jacob, and Jacob would eventually wrestle with God in the desert and get injured. After this event, God changed Jacob's name to Israel. In English, the word "Israel" means to contend with God. Jacob/Israel had 12 sons, who each of the 11 tribes of Israel were named after. The twelfth tribe, at Jacob's request, was named after his son Joseph's two sons, Manasseh and Ephraim.

The temple was built in 957 BC by Solomon and stood until 586 BC. The temple was destroyed by the Babylonians when Nebuchadnezzar II conquered the kingdom of Judah and forced many of the Israelites to go to Babylon. Subsequently, Cyrus II of Persia conquered Babylon in 538 BC. After his conquest of Babylon, Cyrus II allowed the exiled Israelites to return to Jerusalem and rebuild the temple.

Work on the Second Temple was completed in 515 BC [19] The new temple was more modest than the original one and was missing many of the artifacts, most notably the Ark of the Covenant. Where the Ark of the Covenant is today remains a mystery.

In 169 BC, the temple was once again plundered, this time by an offshoot of the Greek empire, and a statue of Zeus was placed in the temple. The placement of Zeus infuriated the Jewish populace and caused the Jewish people to revolt, led by Judas Maccabaeus, who won back Jerusalem and the surrounding area.

In 167 BC, the temple was ritually cleansed and rededicated, without the statue of Zeus. Today, this rededication event is remembered during the holiday called Hanukkah.

It was only later after the first Roman client king, Herod the Great, ruled the area, that major renovations took place, turning the

Second Temple into a grander building and creating the iconic visual which we recognize from ancient images today.

Nicodemus Wonders

Not all in leadership failed to recognize the greatness in Jesus. When Monday night fell, Nicodemus, a member of the Sanhedrin, secretly visited Jesus. Nicodemus wasn't ready to embrace Caiaphas's perspective on Jesus. He often doubted what he heard from Caiaphas and other leaders. If something didn't resonate as true, he investigated. He wasn't someone to blindly follow the crowd, though he was always cautious not to upset Caiaphas.

Nicodemus was well aware of what Caiaphas was like—a person with little empathy for those who opposed him. Opposing Caiaphas was perilous, demanding discretion.

To Nicodemus, there was something intriguing about Jesus. He didn't perceive Jesus as a rogue insurgent but saw him as a thoughtful and compassionate figure. The narrative Caiaphas was peddling about Jesus didn't make sense to him.

Having heard about the resurrection of Lazarus and having witnessed Jesus' widespread adoration and other miracles, Nicodemus found it hard to reconcile Caiaphas's version of Jesus with his own observations.

While Nicodemus was affluent and successful, his life of comfort hindered his quest for the truth. Yet, he felt a powerful need to converse with Jesus. Over the past few years, he had sensed that his life wasn't aligned with God's will. Maybe Jesus had the answers.

As Jesus and the Twelve departed Jerusalem, Nicodemus discreetly trailed them. Once night cloaked the land and ensured his secrecy, he approached Jesus' dwelling. His knock was answered by Jesus, who seemed almost expectant of his visit. Without inquiring about his intentions, Jesus ushered him to a serene spot amidst olive trees.

Nicodemus initiated the conversation. "Rabbi, we know that you are a teacher who has come from God. For no one could perform the signs you are doing if God were not with him" (Jn. 3:2).

Jesus, recognizing sincerity and depth in Nicodemus, replied directly: "Very truly I tell you, no one can see the kingdom of God unless one is born again" (Jn. 3:3).

This answer surprised Nicodemus. Jesus had neither defended himself nor directly acknowledged Nicodemus's observation. Instead, Jesus delved straight into the core of the issue. Nicodemus found himself at a crossroads: one path led to his comfortable, affluent life, and the other demanded full acceptance of Jesus' teachings to truly know God.

In his confusion, Nicodemus asked, "How can someone be born when they are old? Surely they cannot enter a second time into their mother's womb to be born!" (Jn. 3:4). He struggled to grasp Jesus' message of rebirth because he tried to interpret it through a purely logical lens.

Once more, Jesus replied,

> Very truly I tell you, no one can enter the kingdom of God unless they are born of water and the Spirit. Flesh gives birth to flesh, but the Spirit gives birth to spirit. You should not be surprised at my saying, "You must be born again." The wind blows wherever it pleases. You hear its sound, but you cannot tell where it comes from or where it is going. So it is with everyone born of the Spirit. (Jn. 3:5–7)

Jesus spoke with precision. He was not discussing a physical rebirth but rather a spiritual one.

If Nicodemus continued to apply worldly logic and clung to worldly ways, he would fail to experience God spiritually and truly grasp the essence of Jesus.

Nicodemus stood silent in the dim light, his confusion evident to Jesus. Then, Jesus elaborated, "For God so loved the world that he gave his one and only Son, that whoever believes in him shall not perish but have eternal life" (Jn. 3:16).

The significance of Jesus' words was not lost on Nicodemus. He had heard Jesus say that he was from God. Now, he found himself mentally staggering, struggling to assimilate what he had just heard. While Nicodemus was in search of truth, Jesus offered him much more. Intellectually, he grasped Jesus' message, but his comfortable existence hindered his emotional acceptance of it.

True to form, Jesus was succinct with Nicodemus, addressing the pressing question in his mind—what is the truth? Jesus continued, "But whoever lives by the truth comes into the light, so that it may be seen plainly that what they have done has been done in the sight of God" (Jn. 3:21).

Jesus recognized that Nicodemus's plush lifestyle was the primary obstacle to wholeheartedly accepting his words. Yet, it was this very quest for truth that brought Nicodemus to Jesus. Now, equipped with an answer, he needed time for introspection. This encounter marked a pivotal moment for Nicodemus. He was at a crossroads: continue his life of luxury or surmount the formidable challenge of surrendering to Jesus, a decision fraught with potential repercussions, even threatening his very life.

Nicodemus now saw Jesus as preferable to Caiaphas. However, aligning with Jesus came at a significant cost. Other leaders, too, disagreed with Caiaphas. Yet, their readiness to yield to Jesus was not imminent. Unlike Nicodemus, their reservations stemmed from fear, keeping them silent. Like him, though, they were intrigued by Jesus, yet they lacked the audacity to seek him out.

Nicodemus, like many before and after him, faced a monumental choice: to relinquish all in service to Jesus or not. At this juncture, he was hesitant to commit his life fully to Jesus. Departing from his meeting, Nicodemus remained in a quandary over his path forward, but he was certain of one thing: Caiaphas was gravely mistaken.

Setting the Trap

Soon after Jesus confronted the merchants and moneychangers, Caiaphas and the other leaders convened at his palace. Caiaphas's patience, once cool and calculated, had now reached its limit. He announced to the group, "The time has come for us to kill Jesus."

The leaders had observed how the populace had revered Jesus just the day before. And now, following the incident in the Courtyard of the Gentiles, Jesus had disrupted a significant source of their revenue.

Rather than acknowledging the teachings and miracles of Jesus, Caiaphas and the temple leaders viewed him primarily as an obstacle to their wealth and dominance. Moreover, they perceived him as endangering the fragile peace they had crafted, a peace which ensured minimal Roman interference. Their insatiable greed and ambition blinded them to the true nature and mission of Jesus, leaving them both enraged and desperate.

Caiaphas and the temple authorities had become emblematic of those who lived in defiance of God. The apostle Paul articulates such a state in Romans, stating, "They did not honor God or give thanks to him, but their thinking became futile, and their foolish hearts were darkened" (Rom. 1:21).

Initially, Caiaphas and the religious elite believed they could discreetly dispose of Jesus, just as they had with others who claimed to be the Messiah. But Jesus was no ordinary figure, and it dawned upon them that they had grossly underestimated him. The day's events had been a blow to their pride and wealth. Jesus had publicly defied them, dismantling a lucrative enterprise right before their eyes.

Delay was no longer an option. Caiaphas had promptly convened with the religious leaders at his palace to strategize on neutralizing the "Jesus dilemma." As discussions ensued in his courtyard, they brainstormed various solutions. Caiaphas recognized that prolonged inaction would erode his influence over the elite and clergy.

After much deliberation, they settled on a tactic: they would ensnare Jesus into uttering blasphemy. In doing so, they hoped to unmask him as a fraud, thereby convincing the public that he was no different from past impostors. Ideally, they might even provoke Jesus into making incriminating statements against the Romans.

From this point, the consensus among Caiaphas and the religious leaders was clear: patience had been counterproductive. It was time to act against Jesus—and swiftly.

Now, more than ever, Caiaphas and the temple authorities were prepared to take any measures necessary to permanently remove Jesus from the scene.

3

A FAILED TRAP

Nissan 12 (Tuesday, March 31, 33 AD)

The Withered Fig Tree

IT WAS TUESDAY MORNING, AND JESUS, ACCOMPANIED BY the Twelve, made his way toward Jerusalem once more. Today's mission was distinct; Jesus was aware that he would face questions designed to ensnare him. A single error in his answers could lead to an accusation of blasphemy and his subsequent arrest.

Upon entering the city with the Twelve, Jesus anticipated it would be swarming with religious authorities awaiting his arrival. These were leaders who believed they could handle Jesus. Their confidence didn't stem from an understanding of God's ways but from an inflated sense of their own intellect. For Jesus, this day provided another opportunity to further validate his identity and unveil God's true nature.

As they proceeded, they once again passed the fig tree Jesus had rebuked the day before. To Peter's astonishment, the tree had withered all the way to its roots. He was perplexed by how swiftly this had occurred.

Peter, often seen as the de facto leader of the Twelve due to his directness and distinct mannerisms, was typically the first to respond to Jesus and freely express his views. The others admired him, seeing him as worldly but not domineering, much like an older brother. Even when he wasn't entirely correct, Peter exuded confidence, often posing questions to Jesus or stating his viewpoint, while others hesitated.

Drawing Jesus' attention to the withered tree, Peter expressed his amazement. Jesus replied to Peter and the rest:

> Have faith in God. Truly I tell you, if anyone says to this mountain, "Go, throw yourself into the sea," and does not doubt in their heart but believes that what they say will happen, it will be done for them. Therefore, I tell you, whatever you ask for in prayer, believe that you have received it, and it will be yours. And when you stand praying, if you hold anything against anyone, forgive them, so that your Father in heaven may forgive you your sins. (Mk. 11:22–26 NIV)

To the disciples, Jesus' answer seemed unrelated to Peter's observation about the tree, leaving them silently questioning the connection between the withered tree and faith.

The underlying message escaped them. Jesus intended to convey that just as the tree's rapid withering surpassed human understanding, they should place their faith in him rather than human logic. The essence of his lesson was that by living in accordance with God's ways and wishes, they could realize their hearts' desires.

Furthermore, the withering of the fig tree symbolically forewarned those who had defiled the temple. To Jesus, the leaders of Jerusalem, including Caiaphas, resembled barren fig trees, unfruitful for God's kingdom.

The fig tree also represented the virtue of service. Just as a fig tree's purpose is to bear fruit, Jesus hoped the Twelve would find fulfillment in fruitful service. Their duty was to serve and yield spiritual fruit; without this, true peace would remain elusive.

Jesus emphasized that genuine peace and joy stemmed from serving God and one's neighbors. Only through such service would they uncover profound happiness. The lesson of the withered fig tree was clear: without a commitment to service, one would eventually wither from within.

Humanity's purpose, Jesus believed, was to love God wholeheartedly and to extend that love to one's neighbors. In this dual service lies unparalleled joy—a joy that elevates the soul and infuses life with divine purpose.

After reflecting on the lesson of the withered fig tree, Jesus and the Twelve resumed their ascent to Jerusalem. A palpable tension gripped the Twelve as they pondered the unfolding drama with Jerusalem's leaders. Would Jesus be seized? Could the masses continue shielding him? And were they, his followers, also at risk?

The previous evening, a meeting was held involving Caiaphas, the other priests, scribes, Pharisees, the Sanhedrin, and all the senior leaders of Jerusalem. Their goal: to conspire against Jesus. Uncertain about his return but suspecting it was imminent, they stationed spies to promptly relay any sightings. Once alerted, Caiaphas would inform the priests, scribes, Pharisees, and Sadducees, who would then confront Jesus, aiming to verbally corner him.

Similar to the day before, Jesus and his disciples entered Jerusalem through the Golden Gate. Their arrival, perhaps sooner than Caiaphas had anticipated, was soon detected. Spies quickly spread the word: "Jesus is in town!"

The Priests Attempt to Trap Jesus

As soon as Jesus walked to the Courtyard of the Gentiles, crowds surrounded him, and he began teaching them. Not long after, the priests and scribes came up to Jesus. They aggressively pushed their way to the front of the crowd surrounding Jesus and soon had him encircled. This caused Jesus to stop teaching and look at those who had pushed their way to the front. He knew this was the beginning of a long parrying with those looking to kill him.

They said to Jesus, "By what authority are you saying and doing these things? And who gave you this authority?" (Mk. 11:28).

Jesus knew if he said "heaven" or "God," while what he was saying was true, it would give them the opportunity to arrest him for blasphemy. If he said he was speaking on human authority, then the onlookers would see he was no more than an impostor. Instead of answering their question, Jesus turned the question back on them.

Jesus looked at his questioners, his eyes narrowing and his brow furrowed. To those questioning him, he said, "I have one question, and if you answer the question, I will tell you the answers. John's baptism—was it from heaven or of human origin? Tell me!" (Mk. 11:29–30).

The scribes and the priests discussed it among themselves and said,

> If we say, "From heaven," he will ask, "Then why didn't you believe him?" But if we say, "Of human origin ..." (They feared the people, for everyone held that John really was a prophet.) (Mk. 11:31–32)

Jesus had them trapped; finally, they responded, "We don't know" (Mk. 11:33) To which Jesus replied, "Neither will I tell you by what authority I am doing these things" (Mk. 11:33).

Jesus had stumped them with his simple but elegant response. The priests who were sure they could corner Jesus into either saying something blasphemous or revealing to the crowd he was a phony had failed. The priests and scribes who were supposed to be knowledgeable were the ones exposed.

The priests who had come to question Jesus had a long spiritual heritage. To become a high priest, one had to be a descendant of the tribe of Levi. For instance, Moses and his brother Aaron were descendants of the Levite tribe. When Moses led Israel out of Egypt, with him went the 12 tribes of Israel, of which the Levites were one.

Most priests had long ago given up their God-given mission of serving; instead, they had built a life of being served. No longer was their religious guidance pure; instead, they were politically motivated to stay in power. They had stopped helping the people understand the ways of God. In turn, the people they were supposed to serve stopped listening to them.

There were many priests in this group who questioned Jesus. In the first century, 60 priests likely helped run the temple.[20] They represented an imposing group steeped in religious knowledge. But for Jesus, they were no more than a group of lost souls, enamored more with their high social status than they were with finding and living according to the ways of God.

The scribes who had accompanied the priests were, in modern terms, half-lawyer and half-scriptural experts. They spent their lives drawing up legal documents and rewriting the scrolls of the existing scriptures. Because the scrolls were made of plant-based materials, they only lasted a short time and had to be periodically rewritten. In fact, some scribes would spend a lifetime repeatedly rewriting the same scroll.

Over time, the scribes also became interpreters of scripture and, like the Pharisees, were very legalistic. This was directly opposed to Jesus, who taught to follow the scriptures with holiness and purity and to also have a heart pointed to God and loving neighbors.

Jesus was a threat to the priests and scribes because of his scriptural knowledge. In other words, they now had real competition. Because of his divinity, Jesus' knowledge of scripture was complete and pure. And Jesus was not motivated by power and greed, as were the scribes and the priests. He had the advantage of knowing the real truth.

Jesus had outwitted both the priests and the scribes. Their cockiness was now subdued. Embarrassed, they started to walk away, but Jesus wasn't done talking with the priests and the scribes. Speaking loud enough for them to hear, he started to tell a parable:

A man planted a vineyard. He put a wall around it, dug a pit for the winepress and built a watchtower. Then he rented the vineyard to some farmers and moved to another place. At harvest time he sent a servant to the tenants to collect from them some of the fruit of the vineyard. But they seized him, beat him, and sent him away empty-handed. Then he sent another servant to them; they struck this man on the head and treated him shamefully. He sent still another, and that one they killed. He sent many others; some of them they beat, others they killed.

He had one left to send, a son, whom he loved. He sent him last of all, saying, "They will respect my son." But the tenants said to one another, "This is the heir. Come, let's kill him, and the inheritance will be ours." So, they took him and killed him, and threw him out of the vineyard.

What then will the owner of the vineyard do? He will come and kill those tenants and give the vineyard to others. Haven't you read this passage of Scripture:

> The stone the builders rejected
>   has become the cornerstone;
> the Lord has done this,
>   and it is marvelous in our eyes?
> (Mk. 12:1–11)

After hearing this, the priests and scribes were enraged to the point of deranged irrationality. They knew the parable had been about them and their plan to kill Jesus. Now they were steaming. Common people didn't talk to them this boldly, but this mere magician had chastised and embarrassed them publicly in front of many.

The priests and scribes angrily wondered, "Who does this man think he is?" After years of quiet acquiescence from the people, Jesus' boldness had caught the priests and scribes off guard. It seemed each time they tried to trap Jesus, he outsmarted them.

The priests went back to Caiaphas and informed him they had not succeeded. Disappointed, he sat down. What frustration! So far, each move he had made to trap Jesus had been repelled.

The Pharisees Attempt to Trap Jesus

Next, Caiaphas sent the Pharisees to trap Jesus. The Pharisees, a tenacious group, would not give up easily. Their fervent zeal would be challenging for Jesus to counter. The Pharisees were a legalistic group, rigidly following what they believed. Interestingly, they didn't adhere solely to scripture, and they selectively followed traditions, especially those aligning with their beliefs and lifestyles.

Consequently, they ensured that everyone witnessed their piety. They paraded their (false) virtue and practiced their piety in public. Instead of genuinely helping others, they virtue signaled without embodying true virtue. They donned long prayer shawls as a symbol of their devotion but rarely prayed with sincere faith.

They often shamed dissenters, using shame as a powerful tool to silence opposition. This frequently involved feigning offense to make the supposed offender feel guilty or unworthy.

When Caiaphas enlisted the Pharisees to ensnare Jesus, he believed their legalistic and precise nature would be effective. Although not influential stakeholders in Jerusalem's power hierarchy, their zealousness and rigidity starkly contrasted Jesus' teachings. While Jesus respected the law and the scripture, he emphasized the importance of heartful devotion. This nuance was lost on most Pharisees, who prioritized manipulating the populace over understanding.

The Pharisees were very argumentative, valuing being correct over seeking truth. Their relentless drive to always be right led them to argue rather than listen. They weren't in pursuit of truth; they sought victories in debates and hoped to uncover flaws in Jesus' teachings.

The Pharisees confronted Jesus in the Courtyard of the Gentiles. With deceptive intent, they inquired, "Teacher, we acknowledge your integrity. You remain impartial, teaching God's ways truthfully. Is it lawful to pay taxes to Caesar?" (Mk. 12:14–15).

Their question aimed to corner Jesus. They hoped he would critique the tax, thus opposing Roman decrees. Any anti-Roman sentiment could lead to Jesus' arrest on charges of treason.

But Jesus discerned their deceit.

"Why test me?" He responded. "Show me a denarius." Examining the coin they provided, he queried, "Whose likeness and inscription is this?"

"Caesar's," they answered.

Jesus proclaimed, "Render to Caesar what is Caesar's, and to God what is God's." (Mk. 12:14–17).

The crowd marveled at Jesus' astute reply, recognizing the Pharisees' failure to ensnare him. Both the priests and the Pharisees had underestimated Jesus, and their plots crumbled in the face of his wisdom.

The Third Attempt to Trap Jesus

After the Pharisees failed, Caiaphas gathered up the Sadducees for a meeting. When they met, the Sadducees took on a tone of superiority and told Caiaphas they would accomplish what the others had failed to do. The Sadducees represented the Jewish aristocrats and held some of the seats on the Sanhedrin.

This group was steeped in religious law but overly confident of their ability to trap Jesus. They were also highly motivated; if they did not succeed, their tightly controlled relationship with Rome and their own extensive landholdings would be in jeopardy.

The Sadducees disliked Jesus not only because he threatened their wealth but also because they believed his teachings gave people false hope.

They were also strict believers in the Torah, the first five books of the modern Bible. Unlike the Pharisees, they did not believe oral tradition was equal to scripture.[21] In terms of free will, interestingly, they believed God had no control over humans; in other words, they believed in unrestrained, human free will. They also used ritualistic practices to justify their control over the temple and the money it generated. In effect, they used ritual purity as a shield for their unholy activities. [22]

They confidently went down to the city and found Jesus. They opened their questioning of Jesus by asking a seemingly inane question about the state of marriage after death. This was an interesting ploy by the Sadducees, as they themselves did not believe there was an afterlife. As a group, they believed the soul died with the body.[23]

They slyly asked,

> Teacher, Moses wrote for us that if a man's brother dies and leaves a wife but no children, the man must marry the widow and raise up offspring for his brother. Now there were seven brothers. The first one married and died without leaving any children. The second one married the widow, but he also died, leaving no child. It was the same with the third. In fact, none of the seven left any children. Last of all, the woman died too. At the resurrection whose wife will she be, since the seven were married to her?" (Mk. 12:19–23)

This appears to be an absurd question, but it wasn't. The question was another attempt to trap Jesus. If he answered the question of whose wife she would be after death, the Sadducees, because of their belief that there was no resurrection, could declare blasphemy.

Instead, Jesus once again turned the question against those questioning him by saying,

> Are you not in error because you do not know the Scriptures or the power of God? When the dead rise, they will neither marry nor be given in marriage; they will be like the angels in heaven. Now about the dead rising—have you not read in the Book of Moses, in the account of the burning bush, how God said to him, "I am the God of

Abraham, the God of Isaac, and the God of Jacob" He is not the God of the dead, but of the living. You are badly mistaken! (Mk. 12:24–27)

By quoting Moses, Jesus got right at the heart of their beliefs. He exposed their lack of knowledge by using Moses and words from the Torah. Moses was widely believed to be the author of the Torah, which the Sadducees held as the bedrock of their religious views. By using both the Torah and Moses to discredit them, Jesus exposed the Sadducees' lack of knowledge and insight about God.

Jesus had also made a powerful statement about God. He said, "He is not the God of the dead." This is both a rebuke of their lack of knowledge about God and an important statement about God. God is a living God, constantly at work helping creation and humankind. God is an ever-present force.

When Jesus was done, the crowd murmured, and the Sadducees were angry at having been embarrassed. The Sadducees left humiliated and unsure of what they would tell Caiaphas.

One of the scribes had become enamored with Jesus. He listened and stayed close while each group tested Jesus. After the exchange with the Sadducees, he boldly went up to Jesus and asked, "Of all the commandments, which is the most important?" (Mk. 12:28).

Jesus, seeing the sincerity in the lone scribe's question, said,

The most important one, is this: "Hear, O Israel: The Lord our God, the Lord is one. Love the Lord your God with all your heart and with all your soul and with all your mind and with all your strength." The second is this: "Love your neighbor as yourself." There is no commandment greater than these. (Mk. 12:29–31)

To add validity to his answer, Jesus quoted directly from the Torah, by saying "Hear, O Israel: The Lord our God, the Lord is one" (Deut. 6:4–5). This phrase was used in the *Shema* prayer devout Jews said in the morning and at night. This would have been a practice the scribe surely knew about and likely practiced.

Upon hearing Jesus say this, the scribe was humbled. Jesus, in turn, replied to the man, "You are not far from the kingdom of God" (Mk. 12:34). After this last exchange, no one had any more questions.

The crowds who had witnessed these attempts were delighted not only at what Jesus had said but also at his brilliance in handling those attempting to trap him. For too long, they had been taught things they didn't agree with, and they had been forced to comply out of fear.

Three: A Sacred Number

Three groups had tried to trip Jesus up, and all had failed. It was a process for Jesus that mirrored his time in the wilderness when he first started his earthly mission. Like the three religious groups, Satan had also tried three times to trick Jesus and had failed as well.

Numbers are important in the Bible, especially the number three. In Hebrew, three is called *sheloshah* and means harmony, new life, and completeness. The number three appears 467 times in the Bible. For those who were used to hearing scripture orally, numbers and knowing their meaning aided their memory.[24] Three is a very sacred number in the Bible.

Because Jesus was visited three times by the religious leaders, it adds a sacredness to these events. Being visited three times was not a coincidence, neither in his encounter with Satan nor with the religious elite of Jerusalem.

Also, the number three is significant in Christian theology, emblematic of the Holy Trinity: the Father, the Son, and the Holy Spirit. This threefold nature of God is a cornerstone of Christian belief.

Jesus Rebukes the Religious Leaders

Jesus confidently stood up to the bullies. The attempts to trap Jesus had backfired, creating an even stronger connection between Jesus and the masses. Caiaphas's plan had not only failed; it created an even stronger belief Jesus was the long-awaited Savior.

With the crowd engrossed in his teaching, Jesus issued important words of caution.

> Watch out for the teachers of the law. They like to walk around in flowing robes and be greeted with respect in the marketplaces and have the most important seats in the synagogues and the places of honor at banquets. They devour widows' houses and for a show make lengthy prayers. These men will be punished most severely. (Mk. 12:38–40)

Jesus got right to the heart of the problem with the priests, scribes, Pharisees, and Sadducees. Driven by greed, they had used God's Word to gain power and wealth. They had become lost souls, and their religiosity was phony.

In his message, Jesus even used the example of their abuse of poor widows to show how corrupt and venal they had become. Jesus knew the truth, and now it had spilled out into full view.

To the everyday person listening, what Jesus said was uplifting. They all knew what was going on but had little they could do to correct these wrongs. Out of fear, they had gone along while silently disagreeing. As Jesus exposed the leaders, their fear ebbed, and they felt empowered.

Those who had been exploiting God and the people had at first cut only small corners in their immorality. Then, driven by greed and the fear of loss, they had extended their corrupt behaviors until they had completely succumbed to their greed. Now, Jesus had exposed them and their descent into manipulation.

The previous two days, Jesus had entered Jerusalem a revered hero and had ruined the money operation in the temple. Now, Jesus had openly insulted and completely exposed Jerusalem's religious leaders. For three straight days Jesus had stirred up the emotions of

hopefulness with the masses but also disdain by the religious leaders.

After these events, Caiaphas and his thugs were going to arrest
him. But just like on the previous two days, the crowds surrounding
Jesus were large, and arresting Jesus in front of so many witnesses
could induce a riot. They decided to wait, but like all bullies, they
would be back.

The Lesson of the Poor Widow

Before Jesus left the temple area, he sat down with the Twelve and
looked across the courtyard to Solomon's Colonnade. He watched
as the people put money into the boxes set up for donations to the
temple. Some of the rich people put in large amounts and made sure
the onlookers could see their generosity.

A poor widow, hunched over from the burdens of her life, shuffled quietly to the box. She reached into her small purse, which was
attached to her cloth belt, and pulled out two very small coins. She
put the coins in the box and made a small pious gesture. Her faith in
God showed through her eyes as she looked up to the sky. Then she
shuffled quietly away.

Widows in the first century were economically and socially dis-
advantaged. They had few rights as their property was tied to their
husbands and their male children. When their husbands died, they
had no inheritance or physical protection. Without the support of
their sons, widows would be destitute. In the case of this woman, it
appears she had lost everything when her husband died.

Jesus would often point out that widows, because of their de-
fenselessness, should be given protection and support. He knew the
powerful would take their assets and leave them destitute. In a society with few social and economic safety nets, widows were left help-
less.

Jesus turned to his disciples and said,

Truly I tell you; this poor widow has put more into the treasury than all the others. They all gave out of their wealth; but she, out of her poverty, put in everything — all she had to live on. (Mk. 12:43–44)

The long day was over; Jesus rose from where he was sitting and proceeded back to the Golden Gate. As they were leaving Jerusalem, one of the Twelve turned around and saw the temple bathed in shimmering yellow from the rays of a late day sun. He turned to Jesus and said, "Look, Teacher! What massive stones! What magnificent buildings!" (Mk. 13:1).

In turn, Jesus said, "Do you see all these great buildings? Not one stone here will be left on another; every one will be thrown down" (Mk. 13:2). Quizzically, the Twelve turned around and looked at all the magnificent buildings and wondered how this could possibly happen.

As they were passing through the Golden Gate, Jesus turned and looked at the city. He knew there was more he must do. But he thought to himself, *I have done enough for now!*

4

THE BETRAYAL

Nissan 13 (Wednesday, April 1, AD 33)

CAIAPHAS WAS NOW DESPERATE. HE SAT QUIETLY IN HIS house, unable to sleep the previous night. It seemed whatever he tried failed, and Jesus always outsmarted him. He was now frantic, as his thoughts darted back and forth. He knew he was no longer in control—Jesus was.

Annas, his father-in-law, came to visit early in the morning and was worried as well. Much of what Annas had built over the last 24 years was at risk, and he could tell Caiaphas was no longer in control. He sat down, looked directly at Caiaphas and curtly said, "You need to get this Jesus thing under control; you are on the brink."

Caiaphas sighed and now realized even Annas had lost faith in him. Struggling to find his words, he sheepishly assured Annas not to worry. He would soon have everything resolved, perhaps even today. Annas was skeptical and told Caiaphas to keep him updated on his next moves.

Almost three decades earlier, Annas had become the high priest and leader of the Sanhedrin. After holding the position for nine years, he handed the reins over to Caiaphas. Because of Caiaphas's cunning and strategic patience, Annas had seen him as a worthy successor. For the previous 15 years, Caiaphas had proven him right, but now Jesus was slowly undermining Caiaphas. Many members of the Sanhedrin also began to question Caiaphas's leadership.

As the leader of the Sanhedrin, Caiaphas knew he had to address the Jesus situation immediately. Not only was his income at risk, but the aristocrats and religious leaders were growing anxious. In this moment, Caiaphas felt he was rapidly losing influence over Rome and Jerusalem.

Caiaphas had observed that the pilgrims who had come to Jerusalem for the Passover holiday and the locals were captivated by Jesus. Many truly believed he was the long-awaited Messiah, the one to rescue them from their dire circumstances. Jesus was diminishing his authority right before his eyes.

Jesus had been outmaneuvering him. The three groups sent to deceive Jesus had all failed. In fact, Jesus' answers to their attempts only further encouraged the masses to believe in him. For Caiaphas, the previous day had been a tremendous setback; Annas's visit only solidified what Caiaphas had been feeling.

Regrettably, Caiaphas overlooked a simpler resolution to his problem. He could have acknowledged the reality that Jesus was the Messiah they had been waiting for. Had he curbed his lust for power and sought genuine truth, he would have found the answer. He also failed to realize that Jesus' purpose was to serve, not to be served — a stark contrast to how Caiaphas lived.

Caiaphas believed true power meant having others serve him. He failed to see that when those around him showed loyalty, it was merely a facade. They weren't genuinely loyal to Caiaphas; they were merely trying to stay in his good graces to evade punishment or to gain material benefits. Blind to the masses' intelligence and ability to see through his schemes, like many arrogant leaders, Caiaphas had crafted a distorted reality for himself.

After Annas departed, Caiaphas's mood darkened further. He summoned a servant to his sitting area. Upon the servant's arrival, he berated him for not preparing a satisfactory breakfast. He verbally threatened to dismiss him and even imprison him — all over an unsatisfactory breakfast. In this moment, Caiaphas's true nature was revealed: he was utterly devoid of decency.

Now frantic, his evil nature had completely taken over. His singular goal in this situation was to kill Jesus. He believed that if he had Jesus arrested and executed, he would be free of him for good. However, Jesus now had the unwavering support of the masses, who would likely revolt if any harm befell him. He was in a tightly closing trap. After the servant left, Caiaphas buried his face in his hands, his mind racing with thoughts and concerns.

Caiaphas realized that capturing Jesus could instigate a revolt, endangering the fragile alliance with Rome. Such a revolt would provoke a swift and severe response from Rome, endangering him and the religious elites.

He understood that the Roman occupiers employed different administrative structures across their conquered territories. The entire Roman Empire spanned 75 million people, with Rome itself housing just one million.[25] To exert strict control over all the territories would strain their resources, so they typically governed regions that remained peaceful and paid taxes with a lighter touch.

However, if a region caused trouble, the Romans acted swiftly, often adopting a scorched-earth policy. This approach served dual purposes: it subdued the troublesome territory and acted as a warning to other regions about the consequences of resistance. One notable display of this brutal strategy occurred in 146 BC when Carthage was decimated by the Romans. In the aftermath of the conflict, the population of 250,000 was slashed to a mere 50,000. The survivors were sold into slavery, and the city was leveled. This viciousness was the cost of defiance.[26]

Caiaphas was acutely aware of this history and the immediate threat Jesus posed. He envisioned the potential devastation in Jerusalem and his inevitable downfall. The idea of his own children being sold as slaves in distant lands was terrifying.

He also thought about the aristocrats who had considerable wealth and lands at risk, all of which could vanish if a rebellion erupted. Those in power led relatively comfortable lives. He was convinced they were questioning his ability to maintain control.

At this moment, a panic-stricken Caiaphas felt his influence waning. He got up from his chair, paced back and forth in his palace, frantically contemplating his options. Time was running out, and he needed to act.

Gradually, he devised a strategy: apprehend Jesus under the cover of night and bring him to his palace in Jerusalem before dawn. This would allow for a trial away from Jesus' followers.

He needed to call in favors, requiring enforcers and a group willing to serve as witnesses. Moreover, he needed a justification for arresting Jesus. While fabricated, it had to be plausible to the Romans, particularly to the Roman prefect Pontius Pilate and to Herod Antipas. The arrest had to be based on a perceived violation of religious law, something unfamiliar to the Romans so they wouldn't question it.

Furthermore, Caiaphas believed he could secure the backing of Pilate and Herod if he demonstrated that Jesus posed a threat to them and to Roman authority.

As he contemplated his strategy, he wondered if there was a traitor within Jesus' inner circle. Such a turncoat would make the arrest more straightforward. He recalled hearing about Judas' growing discontent. Perhaps they could persuade him to betray Jesus. Acting on this lead, Caiaphas called for a scribe who was acquainted with Judas.

Upon the scribe's arrival, Caiaphas welcomed him to his sitting room. The two engaged in a hushed conversation about Judas' apparent disillusionment. Eagerly, Caiaphas probed for more information.

The scribe, sensing an opportunity to rise in stature, agreed to approach Judas. As he departed, Caiaphas urged him to act swiftly.

Normally composed and shrewd, Caiaphas was now in turmoil. He felt as though the walls were closing in, his influence over Jerusalem's affairs waning. This new scheme was likely his final hope, and the looming prospect of failure was unbearable.

Simon the Leper's House

On Wednesday, Jesus refrained from entering Jerusalem, recognizing the need to give the situation there time to get calm. In the preceding three days, he had achieved his objectives. He had taught the people about faith and God. He had brazenly confronted the corruption in the temple, challenging the money-changers and livestock merchants. Moreover, He had exposed the corruption of the religious and temple leaders in the eyes of the public.

Jesus understood that it was time for these developments to fully settle in and for Caiaphas to absorb the implications of recent events. Any further actions from Jesus at this point could provoke impulsive reactions from Caiaphas. Jesus had done enough; he had pushed Caiaphas and the other leaders to their limits.

Rather than continue to stir the pot in Jerusalem, Jesus and the 12 apostles opted for a different course. They traveled to visit Simon the Leper, who lived nearby in Bethany.

Upon hearing of Jesus' intent to visit, Simon promptly arranged a dinner in Jesus' honor. Notably, Simon was the father of Martha, Mary, and Lazarus. Lazarus was the man whom Jesus had miraculously brought back to life just a few months earlier.

The fact that Simon the Leper could move about in regular society was itself a miracle.

In ancient Jerusalem, leprosy was viewed as an incurable disease, believed to be highly contagious. It was also perceived as a curse from God, rendering a person spiritually impure according to Jewish traditions. Those diagnosed with leprosy were forced into isolation, often for their entire lives.

In the twenty-first century, leprosy is referred to as Hansen's disease. With modern medicine, it can be cured if detected early. Globally, there are approximately 200,000 cases reported each year, with between 100 to 200 cases annually in the United States.[27]

Leprosy is a debilitating condition, producing severe sores and nerve damage that can deform the hands and feet. In some instances, it can even lead to blindness. While it is infectious, it's not as easily transmittable as once believed in the ancient world. Due to its severe disfigurement, people of the first century shunned those with leprosy, pushing the affected into isolation.

Many wonder, "If Simon was a leper, how could he have hosted a dinner for Jesus?" Although leprosy typically condemned one to lifelong isolation, not all skin conditions were incurable, nor were they always leprosy. Someone might have had severe acne, psoriasis, or an allergic reaction to certain foods or plants. Once the condition improved, there was a process to be declared both physically and spiritually healed.

A person, once labeled a leper but now seemingly healed, could, according to the Book of Leviticus, approach a temple priest for a declaration of healing. This would clear them of being contagious or spiritually impure. While uncommon, this did happen.

Furthermore, Jesus cured lepers during his ministry. The first instance documented in the gospels is after Jesus delivered the Sermon on the Mount. A leper approached him, pleading, "Lord, if you are willing, you can make me clean" (Matt. 8:2). Jesus reached out, touched him, and said, "I will; be clean!" (Matt. 8:3). Instantly, the man was cleansed. Jesus then directed him. "See that you say nothing to anyone, but go, show yourself to the priest and offer the gift that Moses commanded, as a testimony to them" (Matt. 8:4). This directive indicates the existence of a healing confirmation process in first-century Jerusalem.

Simon, cured by Jesus, had also sought a priest's confirmation of his healing. So, why do the gospels still refer to him as "Simon the Leper"? And how did Simon and his family become so close to Jesus? These are intriguing aspects of the Bible, urging us to delve deeper.

"Simon" was the most popular male name in first-century Jerusalem. Since surnames were rare, distinguishing nicknames were essential. Besides Simon the Leper, the gospels mention Simon the Pharisee, who is frequently mistaken for Simon the Leper. Although both hosted dinners for Jesus, differences in the respective events make them unlikely to be the same person. Among Jesus' disciples, there were two Simons: Simon (renamed Peter by Jesus) and Simon the Zealot.

"Simon the Leper" served as a unique identifier, albeit an unflattering one. Another revelation is that Simon the Leper was the father of Martha and Mary, known from the resurrection of their brother, Lazarus. Jesus was familiar with Martha and Mary, early disciples, but the gospels don't clarify why. Their significance makes one ponder their initial encounter with Jesus. Instead of chalking it up to mere happenstance, more investigation—exegesis—is required.

It's plausible that Jesus, after healing Simon of leprosy, endeared himself to the siblings: Mary, Martha, and Lazarus. Witnessing such a miracle likely propelled them to become early followers.

This context explains why Simon the Leper and his family were close to Jesus, and why Jesus chose to visit their home in Bethany on the Mount of Olives during a pivotal week. Although it may have seemed like a day of rest, with Jesus, there was always a higher purpose. By day's end, fate's wheels began to turn.

Judas Conspires

When Jesus arrived at Simon's house, he found a comfortable place to recline at the table. The table was like most tables in Jerusalem, low to the ground and surrounded by cushions on three sides. As was the custom, Simon (the host) sat on the center cushion, and Jesus sat on his left. For the first time this week, Jesus was not surrounded by crowds and was able to have a conversation with a close friend.

For the Twelve, this should have been a day of rest, surrounded by friends. However, the Twelve were anxious—they had seen how Jesus had taken the Jerusalem elite to the brink. An unsettled feeling reigned over them as they feared for Jesus and for themselves. Jesus, in his humanity, was also unsettled, but in his divinity, he was sure of his path.

As they sat talking, a woman who had heard Jesus was at Simon's house barged in without an invitation, carrying an alabaster jar of very expensive perfume. The perfume, which contained nard, had a pleasant smell.

Along with being surprised by the interruption, the dinner guests wondered why the woman brought perfume with her. Nard was another term for lavender and was used to anoint a body for burial.

The woman appeared anxious. Finally, she got to see Jesus. Her eyes filled with tears. When she had heard Jesus was at Simon's house, she had felt a strange but wonderfully compelling feeling to go see Jesus and anoint him.

Before anyone could stop her, she abruptly broke open the jar and poured the perfume on Jesus' head.

The people in the room—the Twelve, Simon, his family, and his neighbors—were stunned by what had just happened. The perfume was very expensive and was worth a year's pay. Most in the room rebuked the woman because the perfume could have been sold and the money given to the poor. Upon hearing this, Jesus said,

> Leave her alone. Why are you bothering her? She has done a beautiful thing to me. The poor you will always have with you, and you can help them any time you want. But you will not always have me. She did what she could. She poured perfume on my body beforehand to prepare for my burial. Truly I tell you, wherever the gospel is preached throughout the world, what she has done will also be told, in memory of her. (Mk. 14:6–9)

Jesus' statement confused those in the room. They thought the valuable perfume could have been used to help the poor, but Jesus' statement seemed so contrary to his teachings and normal behavior.

Instead, Jesus knew the perfume was a symbolic part of the burial process for his upcoming crucifixion. Those in the room had heard Jesus talk about his impending death but had either ignored it or simply not understood what he was saying. Because of this, they failed to connect the value of the expensive perfume with the anointing of Jesus' body.

One of the most vocal dissenters was Judas. Entrusted with managing the funds for Jesus and the Twelve, his responsibilities included covering travel expenses and donations to the poor. However, Judas had ulterior motives; he knew that adding the proceeds from the perfume sale would have offered him another opportunity to secretly take a portion for himself.

Though tasked with safeguarding their funds, Judas couldn't resist siphoning off some for personal gain. The allure of being the money keeper led him down a path of deception and theft. Initially, he skimmed only small amounts, convincing himself it was a justified entitlement. But as time passed, his thefts became more audacious, and his justifications grew bolder.

In the Gospel of John, it says about Judas' disapproval concerning the woman who anointed Jesus: "He did not say this because he cared about the poor but because he was a thief; as keeper of the money bag, he used to help himself to what was put into it" (Jn. 12:6). Essentially, Judas' vice was thievery, and he perceived the perfume as yet another means to boost the ministry's funds—a portion of which he intended to divert for his use.

There's another explanation to Judas' questioning of his loyalty to Jesus. Judas did not perceive Jesus as a heavenly messiah destined to save humanity. Instead, he had envisioned Jesus as an earthly leader, one who would rally the masses to overthrow Roman rule in Jerusalem. Judas had hoped he would play a role in this new regime, expecting Jesus to ascend as an earthly king. However, he failed to grasp Jesus' true divine purpose, viewing him instead as indecisive and without clear direction.

In recent months, Judas' conviction that Jesus aimed to be an earthly monarch waned. The more Jesus spoke of heavenly matters in abstract ways, the more perplexed Judas became. His ardent desire to be part of an earthly upheaval made it difficult for him to comprehend Jesus' celestial mission. This confusion seeded doubt about whether he had indeed allied himself with a transformative revolutionary.

When Jesus endorsed the woman's lavish gesture, Judas' belief in Jesus as a revolutionary leader reached its breaking point. It was then that he resolved to betray Jesus.

That night, after departing from Simon's residence, Judas informed the others that he was heading into Jerusalem to see a friend. This struck the other eleven apostles as odd as they returned to their lodging near Gethsemane with Jesus.

Upon reaching Jerusalem, Judas, filled with resentment, coincidentally sought out an old friend who was a scribe. The same scribe that Caiaphas had consulted earlier. Aware that the scribe had close ties to the Sanhedrin and Caiaphas, Judas believed he could leverage his association with Jesus.

Navigating Jerusalem's dimly lit streets, he eventually located the scribe. Recognizing Judas, the scribe, with evident eagerness, led him into a secluded alleyway for a discussion. The scribe quickly discovered the depth of Judas' disillusionment with Jesus. After listening to Judas, the scribe offered to facilitate a meeting with Caiaphas and the temple authorities. Judas consented.

They made their way to Caiaphas's residence. Adopting a cordial demeanor, Caiaphas swiftly persuaded Judas to collaborate in their scheme against Jesus. Seizing the moment, Judas, driven by greed, demanded compensation for his role. Caiaphas, relieved his plan was taking shape, readily promised Judas thirty silver coins, equivalent to roughly 10,000 dollars in today's currency.

For Caiaphas, this development marked a turning point in his battle to defeat Jesus. Relief replaced his earlier desperation, prompting him to strategize further. He was no longer unsure but sure. Needing time to finalize his plans, he asked Judas to return the subsequent evening for a detailed briefing.

What had commenced as a peaceful day for Jesus spent among friends concluded with an act of treachery.

5

THE LAST SUPPER

Nissan 14 (Thursday, April 2, AD 33)

WHEN JESUS AWOKE ON THURSDAY MORNING, IT was an important day for people of the Jewish faith. It was the first day of the Festival of Unleavened Bread and the day to sacrifice the Passover lamb and prepare the Passover meal.

Many had traveled to Jerusalem to celebrate the festivals. Some from neighboring towns and others from places far away. In fact, it was quite common for people from Northern Africa to travel more than a thousand miles to celebrate Passover in the Holy City.[28] On this day, the city would be filled with locals and traveling pilgrims.

For Jesus, it would be a day of preparing the Twelve and himself for the inevitable.

Upon seeing Jesus awake, Peter and John asked him, "Where do you want us to go and make preparations for you to eat the Passover?" (Mk. 14:12). In response, Jesus asked them to go into Jerusalem and gave them these directions,

> Go into the city, and a man carrying a jar of water will meet you. Follow him. Say to the owner of the house he

enters, 'The Teacher asks: Where is my guest room,
where I may eat the Passover with my disciples?" He
will show you a large room upstairs, furnished and
ready. Make preparations for us there. (Mk. 14:13–15)

Upon hearing Jesus' instructions, Peter and John went into Jerusalem. They were two of his closest disciples, and since the beginning, Jesus had been training Peter to be the "Rock upon which I will
build my church" (Matt. 16:18). When Jesus first met Peter, he
changed Peter's name from Simon to Peter. The name Peter means
"rock."

John was also known as one of the "Sons of Thunder," a reference to his brash and quick enthusiasm; his brother James was the
other "Son of Thunder." Jesus saw beyond their brashness. He knew
John had a deep capacity to be compassionate and had an extraordinary intellect. Among the other apostles, John's strong intellect was
respected, but all wished he would soften his mannerisms. In time
and by following Jesus, John would be transformed and, later in life,
become known as the "Son of Love."

The two of them walked the two miles to Jerusalem and entered
the city through the Golden Gate. After proceeding through the gate,
they walked south along Solomon's Porch, which bordered the great
temple and the Courtyard of the Gentiles. After a brief walk to the
southern end of the temple complex, Peter and John arrived at a set
of steps and looked south, down into the sections of Jerusalem called
the City of David and the Lower City.

Scanning the crowds, they looked for a man carrying a jar of
water. As they observed the masses, they spotted many men carrying jars of water. The city was teeming with visitors who had come
to the city to celebrate the two holidays—Passover and the Festival
of Unleavened Bread. The crowds were large, which made it seemingly impossible for them to find the man Jesus had told them about.
Confused, the two men looked at each other, wondering how they
would know which water-carrying man might be the right one.

Off to their right and out of their sight, a man carrying water climbed up the steps toward Peter and John. When the man carrying water approached them, he called out, "Shalom!"

Peter and John turned around and looked at the man climbing the steps. Instantly, they knew he was the man Jesus had told them about. In his hands, he carried a jar of water; instead of them finding the man, the man had found them! Peter and John looked at each other, wondering how the man could just appear and know them. Yet here he was, with a smile and a jar of water.

When the man arrived where they were standing, he once again said to them, "Shalom," which was a greeting of peace. To which Peter and John replied, "Shalom aleichem," which means *peace be upon you.* Both Peter and John instantly liked the smiling man.

The man said to them, "Follow me."

The two followed him down the steps and into the city. Down the crowded streets they went, winding their way past houses and shops. The city was alive with people preparing for this important day. They hurriedly followed the man, who moved quickly and confidently through the crowd.

The man turned into an alley with a two-story house at the end. Upon reaching the house, the man knocked on the door. The owner came to the door and said, "Shalom."

The man carrying the jar of water replied, "Shalom aleichem" and, as was the custom, touched the homeowner on the shoulder with his right hand.

Abruptly, John, remembering what Jesus had told them to say, said, "The Teacher asks: where is my guest room, where I may eat the Passover with my disciples?"

The owner, ignoring John's abruptness, smiled knowingly and said, "Follow me."

They walked to the back of the house through a cobblestone courtyard. As they walked, they saw rooms that opened into the courtyard. Along the right wall, they could see stables for the animals. As they proceeded to the back of the house through another room, they saw a set of wooden steps leading to an upper room.

The men climbed the stairs, and when they arrived at the top, Peter and John saw a large room with a low table and cushions surrounding the table. In this upper room, the owner typically entertained his guests, but on this night, it would be used for Jesus. The table was large enough to comfortably seat 15 or so people. Peter thought to himself, *This would be a perfect spot for Jesus to have the Passover meal.*

The table was set for 13 people who could casually recline on the cushions that surrounded the table. A set of fine red terra sigillata pottery was neatly stacked on the table. This type of stoneware was the current trend in Jerusalem. For the Passover meal, only stone tableware could be used to prevent the transmission of impurity during the sacred meal.

The two men saw everything was ready except for the meal. The owner then told Peter and John he had secured a lamb on Sunday, four days prior. Buying the lamb four days early was the custom given to Moses by God many centuries earlier.

Peter and John knew they had a busy day ahead of them. First, they had to go to the local markets and purchase the other ingredients for the meal. While jars of water were already present in the room, they still had to procure bitter herbs, unleavened bread, a fruit-and-nut paste, eggs, and raw vegetables to dip into a tart dressing.

They knew they had to leave immediately to visit the various shops in the marketplace as it would be very crowded. Throngs of people would be making the same preparations for their own Passover meals.

At three o'clock, they would take the lamb to the temple to be slaughtered in front of the priests. The lamb's blood would drip into the basin at the temple. Then, its fat and kidneys would be removed and burned at the altar. Next, a brief ceremony would be performed by the priest. After skinning the lamb, they would bring it back to the house and place it on an open fire to be roasted.

Then, they would roast the lamb to be cooked by seven p.m. In between, they had to place the items from the market on the table. Jesus and the others would arrive around seven p.m., just at sunset.

Around six p.m., Jesus gathered up those who were with him to make the two-mile trip to Jerusalem. As they walked, Jesus looked around. He passed several fig trees, even the one he had cursed. It was a clear spring day, and the surrounding area was filled with spring flowers. Jesus knew this trip into Jerusalem would start the difficult process of redemption for humankind. He also knew there would be many trials to overcome in the next 24 hours. While divinely ready, Jesus' human side was filled with great apprehension.

When Jesus got close to the Golden Gate, he turned around and scanned the countryside, which was filled with green from the trees and the yellowish-brown tinge of soil and rocks. Sunset would occur at seven p.m.; this would be the last time the fully human Jesus would see the Mount of Olives in the daytime.

Jesus had walked slowly toward Jerusalem in a quiet mood; those with him sensed his mood and were quiet as well. They passed through the Golden Gate and walked along Solomon's Porch toward the city. Knowing where the house was already, Jesus followed a path similar to the one Peter and John had walked earlier that day.

When they arrived at the house in the alley, Jesus knocked on the door. A man came to the door and, upon seeing Jesus, repeatedly and excitedly said, "Shalom, shalom, shalom." Jesus warmly grinned at his friend and replied, "Shalom aleichem." Then he placed his right hand on the man's shoulder and thanked him for letting him use his upper room.

The homeowner told Jesus and the other 10 to follow him. As they walked, the man told Jesus about the preparation, speaking so excitedly and quickly he kept stumbling with the words. They moved through the courtyard and saw Peter and John finishing the cooking of the lamb. Now after seven p.m., they all went up to the upper room of the house.

Normally, Jesus, as the host, would have sat down first. Surprisingly, Judas sat down first, taking the best seat. Jesus then sat next to Judas on his right. Interestingly, both Peter and John took the seats considered the lowest and most humble. John sat at the very end of the oval table, to Jesus' right, and Peter sat across from John at the other end of the table.

Those at the meal, also called the Seder, were surprised at Judas' behavior and a little puzzled Jesus had taken his seat so calmly.

The History of Passover

By the time Jesus and the Twelve had reclined on the cushions around the table, the sun had set. With the setting of the sun, the meal could begin. As the Twelve sat with Jesus, he relayed to them the story of Passover. This was an important time for Jesus and the Twelve. In telling the story, he was subtly connecting the past to their present time by connecting Passover to his upcoming crucifixion and resurrection. As the next days unfolded, they would see Jesus was the sacrificial lamb to save them and humankind.

With the exception of Judas, the group was entirely focused on the meaning and purpose of the Passover meal. Judas, though, was silently thinking about his previous night's meeting with Caiaphas and the scribe. He rehearsed in his mind how he would leave the group later that evening and meet with Caiaphas.

Jesus told them the Passover Seder was an important part of remembering the great event that happened in Egypt more than a thousand years earlier.[29] Moses, as instructed by God, had told all the Israelites to sacrifice a lamb and paint the blood of the lamb on their doorways. By doing so, the angel of death would pass over their houses that night.

The Israelites were living in Egypt as slaves at the time. Centuries earlier, they had arrived in Egypt to escape a famine in their own land. At first, they were allowed to farm and live normal lives. But as they grew larger and more prosperous, the pharaoh of Egypt became fearful they were getting too powerful and would take over the entire land. In response, he made all the Israelites slaves and ordered all their male babies to be killed.

Moses, who was born during this time, escaped death. After his birth, his mother hid him in reeds along the Nile River to prevent his murder. He was then discovered and secretly adopted by pharaoh's daughter. Ironically, as a youth, Moses lived a royal life.

Later as an adult, Moses saw an Egyptian beating an Israelite, and he murdered the Egyptian, forcing him to flee to avoid being arrested. While in exile, Moses encountered God at a burning bush. In this encounter, God told Moses to demand pharaoh free the Israelites.

Pharaoh refused to release the Israelites and, therefore, exposed his nation to ten plagues. Each time a plague occurred, Moses would ask that the Israelites be set free, but each time he was denied by pharaoh.

The tenth or final plague was the most dramatic, the killing of all the first-born males in Egypt by the angel of death. To protect the Israelites, God commanded them to paint lamb's blood on a doorway as a sign for the angel of death to *pass over* their house. After this final plague, and after losing his son, pharaoh agreed to allow the Israelites to leave.

They wandered for 40 years in the wilderness before reaching the land God had promised them. The Passover event occurred in the 13th century BC; however, it was not until the fifth century BC that the Israelites formally celebrated this event of Passover on Nissan 14.[30]

Jesus Washes the Apostles' Feet

After Jesus told them the story, they ate the lamb and the other items Peter and John had prepared. As they ate, an awkward silence filled the room. Each was sure Jesus had more to say and wondered what was coming next.

Jesus gestured for a basin of water. The Twelve exchanged curious glances, murmuring amongst themselves. They had gathered for what they thought would be a simple holiday meal, but something deeper seemed to be unfolding.

Peter, always bold and often quick to voice his thoughts, watched as Jesus began to wrap a towel around His waist. "Master," he exclaimed, a tremor of confusion in his voice, "What are you about to do?"

With a gentle smile, Jesus responded, "What I am doing now, you do not understand, Peter. But you will, in time." He then knelt before Bartholomew, taking the Apostle's worn and dusty feet into his hands, and began to wash them. The room fell silent, each man deeply moved by the humility on display.

John, leaning against a wooden post, whispered to James, "We've seen him perform miracles, command the winds, and raise the dead. Yet here he is, attending to our feet as the lowest of servants would." James nodded, tears welling up in his eyes, as the weight of the gesture sank in. The King of Kings, humbling himself to the stature of a servant, exemplified a love deeper than words could convey.

The Blood of the New Covenant

After Jesus had washed their feet, suddenly he again dramatically shifted the mood in the room by saying, "Truly I tell you, one of you will betray me—one who is eating with me" (Mk. 14:17).

Heads turned to Jesus, shocked by his statement. Everyone but Judas searched their minds to consider if it was them. Eleven of the apostles were saddened by Jesus's comment; then, one by one, they all replied, "Surely you don't mean me?" (Mk. 14:19). In turn, Jesus replied,

> It is one of the Twelve ... one who dips bread into the bowl with me. The Son of Man will go just as it is written about him. But woe to that man who betrays the Son of Man! It would be better for him if he had not been born. (Mk. 14:20–21)

After hearing Jesus say this, Judas grew uncomfortable and uneasy on his cushion. He was the one who had shared the bowl with Jesus for dipping the unleavened bread. Frantically, he wondered what Jesus might know.

Judas remained silent, hoping the moment would pass and no further conversation about betrayal would occur. He was embarrassed but did not let it show. Silently, he wanted to leave so he would no longer be twisting inwardly with anxiety.

The room grew uncomfortable—some thought it was Judas Jesus was talking about. Stillness and stiffness filled the air. Not knowing what to do next, the apostles returned to eating their meal, this time in silence.

Then, Jesus stood up and took the bread, which he broke into pieces, and gave it to everyone in the room. When all had received the bread, Jesus said, "Take it; this is my body" (Mk. 14:22).

This moment harkens back to when John the Baptist first saw Jesus. John had been quizzed by the religious leaders as to whether he was the Messiah or a prophet. John the Baptist replied, "He is the one who comes after me, the straps of whose sandals I am not worthy to untie" (Jn. 1:27).

Later, when John the Baptist saw Jesus walking, he said, "Look, the Lamb of God, who takes away the sin of the world!" (Jn. 1:29). This statement, made at the beginning of Jesus's earthly mission, is directly connected to the Passover lamb, but it is also connected to the crucifixion and its purpose. Jesus' body would be broken during the crucifixion for all believers to share. Symbolically, Jesus was also the Passover lamb, who would save and redeem those who believe in him.

While the Twelve were trying to understand Jesus' comment about the bread and his body, Jesus picked up a cup of wine and said,

> Drink from it, all of you. This is my blood of the covenant, which is poured out for many for the forgiveness of sins. I tell you, I will not drink from this fruit of the

vine from now on until that day when I drink it new
with you in my Father's kingdom. (Matt. 26:28–29)

Jesus drank from the cup and gave it to John, who also drank
from it. John passed it to the right. And on the cup went, passed to
the person on the right. Finally, Judas received the cup and drank
from it as well.

The statement "this is my blood of the covenant" draws parallels with the Old Testament or the Hebrew Bible. The concept of a
covenant was introduced by God when he pledged land and a future to Abraham and his lineage.

In biblical terms, a covenant signifies an agreement God forms
with his people. Not limited to Abraham, God also made covenants
with figures like Moses and Noah. While the Twelve might have
grappled with Jesus' words, they paid close attention. Jesus was ushering in a new covenant, offering forgiveness of sins and a renewed
life to believers.

In the present day, the bread and wine are similar to this inaugural communion. It is our affirmation of belief in both the crucifixion and the resurrection.

Though Jesus initiated the first communion, its significance remained elusive to those present. They struggled with concepts like
being "poured out for many" and Jesus' vow of abstaining from
drink until the advent of God's new kingdom. Their comprehension,
however, was on the horizon.

Jesus then led them in a final hymn and ended the meal. They
all rose from the table and headed back to Bethany and the Mount
of Olives.

On their way to the Mount of Olives, Jesus made another startling comment by saying,

You will all fall away for it is written: "I will strike the
shepherd, and the sheep will be scattered." But after I
have risen, I will go ahead of you into Galilee. (Mk.
14:27–28)

Upon hearing this, Peter protested and said, "Even if all fall away on account of you, I will not" (Matt. 26:33).

Jesus knew what was coming in a matter of hours and knew Peter did not fully understand what he was saying. He also knew Peter would try to stay strong and help Jesus but would later fail to comply. To help Peter understand when the events did occur, Jesus made a prediction: "Truly I tell you, today—yes, tonight—before the rooster crows twice you yourself will disown me three times" (Mk. 14:30).

Still defiant and without thinking, Peter replied, "Even if I have to die with you, I will never disown you." And all the others said the same (Mk. 14:39).

This was an easy statement for Peter and the others to make because they were not yet threatened.

Jesus knew the fragility of the human condition.

6

A FATEFUL EVENING

Nissan 15 (Late Thursday Evening,
April 3, AD 33)

I N ANCIENT JERUSALEM, THE NEW DAY STARTED WHEN
the sun went down.[31] While Jesus and the Twelve had celebrated
Passover in the upper room, the day had changed over from
Thursday to Friday, Nissan 15.

After dinner, they left the room, and Jesus' mood was somber.
He knew the next few hours would be very difficult; his humanity
was wrestling with his divinity. His mind was anxiously searching
for a different way to accomplish the task ahead. In his humanness,
Jesus was desperately considering many options, trying to find a
way to comply with God's will without having to suffer. He was
torn between what he didn't want to do and what he knew he had
to do.

When the group reached the foot of the Mount of Olives at the
border of the Garden of Gethsemane, Jesus turned to some of the
Twelve and said, "Sit here while I pray" (Mk. 14:32). He then turned
to his closest apostles—Peter, James, and John—and asked them to
follow him into the Garden of Gethsemane.

The entrance into Gethsemane was a collection of olive tree groves; some of the trees were hundreds of years old. In the darkness, their torches outlined thick trunks and dense green branches. Through the dim light, they could see what looked like a labyrinth created by the trees. Each tree had an extensive root system, which went deep into the ground to help the trees to soak up what little water existed.[32]

Jesus, with Peter, James, and John, went into the labyrinth of the olive trees. As they walked, Jesus' anxiety grew further, and he became more troubled. He was breathing heavily, at times gasping and shuddering when he was confronted with the reality of his immediate future. Finally, he stopped, bent over, and took a deep breath. Jesus then told Peter, James, and John, "My soul is overwhelmed with sorrow to the point of death ... Stay here and keep watch" (Mk. 14:34).

Jesus walked further into the grove of trees by himself. Overwhelmed by his human fear, he went to his knees, and each time he thought about his future, he trembled. He was consumed with anxiety.

Finally, he began to pray. In his prayer, he sought another way. His mind was filled with many competing thoughts, but mostly, he just wanted to find a different way because he knew the pain that was coming. His eyes were clenched, and his face was contorted; he desperately sought clarity and an end to his confusion.

Then, lifting his head heavenward, he said, "*Abba*, Father, everything is possible for you. Take this cup from me. Yet not what I will, but what you will" (Mk. 14:35). This prayer revealed his inner struggle. In his humanity, he wanted a safer way to complete his task, to avoid the painful drama that was coming. Yet in his divine state, he knew God had a plan and trusted God.

He rose from the ground, feeling somewhat relieved, and walked back to where he had left Peter, James, and John. Stunningly, when he arrived at the spot where he had left them, Jesus found them asleep, oblivious to the cosmic struggle he was undergoing. He needed them, but they had succumbed to their fatigue. Jesus woke Peter and said,

> Simon, are you asleep? Couldn't you keep watch for one hour? Watch and pray so that you will not fall into temptation. The spirit is willing, but the flesh is weak. (Mk. 14:37–38)

Jesus needed Peter. In his disappointment, he had addressed Peter by his former name, symbolizing how Peter had drifted away while Jesus was grappling with mental anguish. Dismayed, Jesus turned and retreated into the grove.

Once more, his knees grew weak, and his breath became labored. Confronted again with the daunting reality of his imminent fate, he fell to his knees to pray. Sweat, born from his inner turmoil, dripped from Jesus' face. Torn between God's design for him and his human longing to find another way, he fervently sought clarity. In his mind, the same plea continually formed: "Not my will but yours."

This internal battle persisted. While he recognized the necessity of following God's plan, his human nature gave way to doubt. Each time he felt prepared, dread overwhelmed his humanity. And so, the struggle endured.

After some time, Jesus stood and approached the trio. To his dismay, he found them sleeping once more. Overcome by fatigue, their eyelids were heavy. In this moment, Jesus realized the depth of his solitude in this conflict.

For a third time, he ventured into the grove. With each passing moment, Jesus' prayers grew more determined. When he finally submitted to God's plan, a newfound clarity arose, and his determination solidified. During his third and concluding prayer, he declared with unwavering conviction, "Yet not as I will, but as you will" (Matt. 26:39). Upon these words, a spirit of resolution enveloped Jesus. He was fortified, prepared to enact the divine blueprint.

His grueling journey to fully accepting his mission had been completed. As Jesus made his way back to the apostles, his stride was firm and unyielding. Upon reaching them, he pronounced:

> Are you still sleeping and resting? Enough! The hour has come. Look, the Son of Man is delivered into the hands of sinners. Rise! Let us go! Here comes my betrayer! (Mk. 14:41–42)

Even though Jesus was the Son of God, he consistently identified himself as the Son of Man, highlighting his commitment to serve humanity. With unwavering resolve, he was set to fulfill his terrestrial mission.

The group of four then returned to those awaiting them at the perimeter of Gethsemane. Serving God and humanity had become Jesus' singular focus.

Judas' Final Betrayal

As the Passover Seder had continued, Judas maintained a remarkably calm facade, despite Jesus having singled him out earlier. Inside, though, his mind was a storm of schemes and choices. When Jesus led the group to the border of Gethsemane and then departed, Judas sensed the moment had ripened. Silently, he slipped away, setting his path back to Jerusalem and towards Caiaphas.

Upon his arrival, Caiaphas greeted Judas with a warmth as deceptive as it was inviting. Consumed by his thirst for the promised reward, Judas was blind to the High Priest's hollow charade and spilled every secret he knew, including the crucial details of where Jesus could be seized. Caiaphas listened intently, especially when Judas recounted any claims Jesus made about divinity, unity with God, or being the prophesied Messiah. In his fervor to secure his prize, Judas' words became tinged with embellishment.

Hope ignited in Caiaphas's eyes. Judas had handed him the perfect opportunity on a silver platter. With the shroud of night as his ally to deter large crowds, Caiaphas felt the urgency of the unfolding moment. It was time to strike.

Acting swiftly, Caiaphas summoned his trusted priests, scribes, and loyal followers. Selecting a handful of individuals to serve as witnesses, he briefed them on Judas' narrative, coaching them on what they would need to recite in the imminent trial. One by one, they eagerly concurred, each envisioning the favors they might gain through their allegiance to Caiaphas's plan.

As the head of the Sanhedrin and the temple, Caiaphas was accustomed to the constant presence of a crowd that feigned loyalty — among them, rough men with a taste for brutality. Armed with this menacing entourage, which included his servant Malchus and Judas himself, Caiaphas dispatched them with clubs and swords to enact the final act of this drama: the arrest of Jesus.

That night, as they moved through the shadows towards their target, the air was thick with tension, every step echoing with the weight of what was to come.

Judas led the way and told the group he would kiss Jesus to make sure they arrested the right person. When they arrived, Jesus was just meeting up with the rest of the group at the edge of Gethsemane. Upon seeing Jesus, Judas went straight to him, said, "Rabbi!" and kissed him.

Seeing this, the thugs quickly grabbed Jesus and put him under arrest. There was much shouting and jostling. Judas, who stood nearby, was startled by the suddenness and brutality of the events. In this dramatic moment he saw the results of his impetuous scheming become very real, and he became unsettled.

Peter, enraged, drew his sword, and cut off the ear of Caiaphas's servant, Malchus.

Jesus glared at Peter and said, "Put your sword away! Shall I not drink the cup the Father has given me?" (Jn. 18:11). After which, in an act of compassion, Jesus touched Malchus, and his ear was healed.

Then Jesus turned to the group, who had seized him and defiantly said,

> Am I leading a rebellion, that you have come out with swords and clubs to capture me? Every day I was with you, teaching in the temple courts, and you did not arrest me. (Mk. 14:48–49)

Jesus looked at the angry thugs holding him. They were waiting to see what would happen next, wondering if Jesus would resist. Jesus then announced, "But the Scriptures must be fulfilled" (Mk. 14:49).

This last comment by Jesus raises immediate questions: What scriptures must be fulfilled? And why is this important? In the four gospels, we do not find a reference to the exact passage Jesus is referring to. So, some detective work must be used to find the scripture Jesus is referencing.

The first clue is that the scripture Jesus is referring must come from the Hebrew Bible, as the New Testament hadn't been written yet at this time. So, it is likely the scripture Jesus was referring to would come from an ancient Hebrew prophet. Another clue relates to the Passover period; it would also likely include a reference to a sacrificial lamb—the sacrificial lamb representing the sacrifice Jesus would be making for all humankind. A final clue is that Jesus did not put up a struggle when his attackers arrived.

When we put these filters in place, a potential candidate is found in Isaiah 53:7, which says:

> He was oppressed and afflicted,
>   yet he did not open his mouth;
> he was led like a lamb to the slaughter,
>   and as a sheep before its shearers is silent,
>   so he did not open his mouth.

When we review other scholars' comments, we find agreement this is the verse or scripture to which Jesus was most likely referring.

Jesus knew his death would erase the sins of the world, and he once again gave in to the mission assigned to him by God. Upon hearing Jesus' resignation and silent willingness to be arrested, those who were with him fled in fear. One of them almost got caught, but fortunately, his garment came off, and the captors were left holding his tunic while he escaped.

The group took Jesus and bound his hands. They walked back to Jerusalem to go to Caiaphas's residence. All those who had arrested Jesus were gleeful at whom they had captured and glad there hadn't been much of a struggle. Their plan had been far easier to accomplish than they had expected.

As soon as Judas saw Jesus bound and being taken away, he began to feel utter remorse, wondering what he had done. The thugs bullied Jesus as they took him up the hill toward Jerusalem; Judas saw Jesus being jostled by the unruly mob and began to wish he hadn't been so petulant.

The group had been told to bring Jesus to Caiaphas's house. His house was in the southwest corner of Jerusalem in an area called the Upper City, a convenient place with a large courtyard surrounding a palatial residence. Additionally, Caiaphas's house was not near the temple. This made it a perfect spot for what was about to take place; not many of the holiday visitors would be nearby to cause trouble.

The Trial

When they arrived at Caiaphas's house, they found him in his courtyard surrounded by many people: scribes, priests, pre-selected witnesses, and most importantly, the 70 members of the Sanhedrin. In a remarkably short period of time, Caiaphas had assembled this group.

Although Caiaphas and the Sanhedrin had the authority to conduct a trial, their decision-making and enforcement powers were limited. This wouldn't be a civil or criminal trial but a religious one. While the Sanhedrin could convene and rule on some issues, their authority was curbed by Rome. Thus, they could only find Jesus guilty of blasphemy or an offense against God. This verdict could be reached either through evidence from two or three witnesses or by a confession from Jesus himself in front of the Sanhedrin.

Caiaphas called on the prearranged witnesses to testify. One stood up and claimed he had heard Jesus say he was the son of David. Another recounted that he had heard Jesus threaten to destroy the temple. Each witness's testimony followed, but their accounts were inconsistent and disjointed. Many seemed to have forgotten parts of their rehearsed lines. Given the contradictory and overly emotional nature of the testimonies, they were deemed inadmissible.

Caiaphas, seeing his plan unravel, grew anxious. Some of Caiaphas's loyalists from the crowd then claimed Jesus had said, "I will destroy this temple made with human hands and in three days will build another, not made with hands" (Mk. 14:58–59). But even these testimonies had discrepancies.

Seeking evidence, Caiaphas probed Jesus, "What is this testimony these men bring against you?" (Mk. 14:60). Jesus chose to remain silent.

Growing impatient, Caiaphas directly challenged Jesus, "Are you the Messiah, the Son of the Blessed One?" (Mk. 14:61).

Without hesitation, Jesus responded, "I am. And you will see the Son of Man sitting at the right hand of the Mighty One and coming on the clouds of heaven" (Mk. 14:62).

The phrase "I am" is a declaration of his divinity. Centuries earlier, God had identified himself to Moses at the burning bush as "I am." Jesus was now asserting the same identity, effectively declaring his divinity to Caiaphas.

Seizing upon Jesus' claim and that he would sit beside the Mighty One, Caiaphas knew he had the evidence he needed. Feigning horror, he theatrically tore his clothes and appealed to the crowd, "Why do we need any more witnesses? You have heard the blasphemy. What do you think?" (Mk. 14:63–64).

Fueled by Caiaphas's fervor, the crowd turned on Jesus with rage. They spat on him, beat him, and blindfolded him. As they dragged him into the cold depths of Caiaphas's basement, their brutality showed no signs of abating. Jesus had been found guilty.

Peter Denies Jesus Three Times

Peter had secretly followed Jesus and his captors back to Jerusalem. While the trial was being held, Peter tentatively stood in the back. As he was standing warming himself over a fire, one of Caiaphas's servant girls noticed him, having previously seen him in the temple with Jesus. Inquisitively, she asked him, "Aren't you the one who was with Jesus?"

Peter replied, "I don't know what you are talking about." Fearing more questions, he quickly left to go to the other side of the crowd. As he walked, a rooster from a nearby house crowed, signaling morning was near. Not willing to give up, the servant girl followed him and announced to those standing around, "This fellow is one of them" (Mk. 14:69).

Peter said, "This is not true!"

Then the others who had started to mill about also asked him, "Surely you are one of them and you are the Galilean" (Mk. 14:70).

After this question, Peter began to curse and wave his arms wildly. Then, for a third time, Peter denied knowing Jesus and said, "I don't know this man, the one you are talking about" (Mk. 14:71).

After Peter made this third denial, the rooster crowed a second time. At the same time, Jesus was being dragged to the basement of Caiaphas's residence. Jesus looked straight at Peter. Then Peter remembered what Jesus had said to him: "Before the rooster crows twice you will disown me three times" (Mk. 14:72).

Despondent, Peter walked away from the crowd, stunned by his failure. Angry at himself, he sought a solitary place to hide. Gasping for breath, he fell to his knees. There, he began to sob, realizing he had once again failed Jesus when he was needed the most.

As Peter sobbed, the sun rose over the horizon.

7

The Lamb Is Sacrificed

Nissan 15 (Friday, April 3, AD 33)

A S THE FIRST RAYS OF DAWN PAINTED THE SKY, A DE-
termined Caiaphas felt the weight of his treacherous scheme.
With Jesus bound and blindfolded, the dawning of a new
day intensified his urgency. The Roman occupiers had to be convinced, and only the enigmatic Pontius Pilate could sanction the
fateful act. Fearful the whispers of Jesus' fate would begin to ripple
through Jerusalem, Caiaphas felt the pressing need to secure Pilate's
nod before the city erupted in chaos.

The members of the Sanhedrin, the unwavering Pharisees, the
scribes, and the temple merchants—they all needed assurance. Time
was of the essence. With many still lurking in the shadows of his
palace following the trial, the air was thick with anticipation. As the
morning unveiled itself, Caiaphas, with a steely resolve, summoned
them. The stakes were high.

Caiaphas would confront Pilate, but he needed an imposing entourage to accentuate the gravity of his plea. His loyalists were crucial for this endeavor. The courtyard echoed with fervent
discussions and footsteps, converging around the formidable figure

of Caiaphas. As the atmosphere tensed, enforcers descended into the cellar, their intentions clear: to bring forth Jesus.

From an historical perspective, Caiaphas's residence is reportedly now called the Church of St. Peter in Gallicantu, meaning, in English, "where the cock has crowed,"[33] this being a reference to Peter's three denials and the rooster crowing. In the lower level is a dungeon carved out of bedrock with a prison cell and guard's room.[34] The courtyard of this house is thought to be where Jesus was tried by Caiaphas. While many archeologists believe this church sits on the site of Caiaphas's palace, it cannot be proven. At the very least, it is today a good representation of the place of the trial of Jesus.

With Jesus brought up from the dungeon in Caiaphas's palace, the group headed toward Pilate's palace and court. Pilate lived in the Antonia Praetorium, where the resident Roman army headquarters were also located. Many years earlier, Herod had built the praetorium and named it after Mark Anthony (Antonia). Herod built the headquarters close to the temple so the Roman army would be close by if any trouble arose there. In fact, two 600 ft. aerial bridges connected the praetorium to the temple.[35]

The path to Pilate took the group along the west wall of Jerusalem near Herod's original palace. Taking this path would keep them away from the outer courts of the temple and the crowds. From there, they would proceed through a gate, which would lead them north along another wall, before turning east toward the praetorium. This route would avoid the temple area until they got close to the praetorium.

When they arrived, Caiaphas demanded that the guard fetch Pilate. Aware of Caiaphas's political stature, the guard promptly went to summon Pilate. After a short while, a visibly irritated Pontius Pilate, inconvenienced by the early summons, appeared from behind two pillars. He was dressed in a cream-colored woolen toga with broad red stripes, and red leather shoes adorned his feet. His attire was consistent with the standards for Roman governors of the first century, standards that Pilate meticulously followed.

Pilate served as the fifth governor and prefect of Judea. With strong political and social connections in Rome, he had secured his position as the prefect, which also made him the head of the small military force in Jerusalem. This force functioned both as an army and a police in Roman territories. Pilate wasn't particularly fond of Jerusalem, but viewed it as a valuable stepping stone for future career moves.

Part of his duties were judicial, granting him the authority for criminal sentencing. He was pragmatic, understanding the need to maintain peace with the local religious authorities. While devoted to Roman deities, Pilate saw no advantage in disturbing local religious customs.

His key to success in Judea was ensuring stability. Even though he personally disliked Caiaphas, Pilate recognized his influence over the Jewish population. As governor, he had the power to dismiss Caiaphas from his position as chief priest. Yet, as long as Caiaphas ensured peace, Pilate would tolerate him.

Upon seeing Caiaphas, Pilate gestured for him to approach. Despite viewing him as a corrupt leader, he recognized the importance of maintaining a civil relationship. Things had been calm recently, and Pilate didn't want to ignite any unnecessary conflicts.

Caiaphas briefed Pilate on Jesus' alleged blasphemy from the previous night and demanded his execution. Hoping to further provoke Pilate, Caiaphas added, "He claims to be a king." Caiaphas was assertive, pushing Pilate for a resolution.

Seeking to placate Caiaphas, Pilate agreed to meet Jesus. He instructed that Jesus be brought to the courtyard. Caiaphas, heeding this command, signaled the guards to escort Jesus.

As Jesus reached the top of the steps, Pilate inquired, "Are you the king of the Jews?"

"You have said so," Jesus replied (Lk. 23:3).

Upon hearing Jesus' response, Caiaphas and the raging crowd accused Jesus of treason, sedition, and agitation.

Pilate, observing Jesus' silence to these allegations, said, "Aren't you going to answer? See how many things they are accusing you of" (Mk. 15:4).

But Jesus remained silent, impressing Pilate with his composure. Pilate had also been forewarned by his wife, who had dreamt about Jesus and advised him to steer clear.

Now face-to-face with Jesus, Pilate was unnerved, torn between his wife's warning and Caiaphas's insistence.

Efforts to prompt Jesus to speak were futile. Pilate was familiar with tales of Jesus assisting the Judean populace. Now, with Caiaphas pressing for Jesus' execution, Pilate realized that this just might be a ploy to eliminate competition. Remembering his wife's advice, he was inclined to release Jesus.

Assertively, he told Caiaphas that he found no charge against Jesus. But Caiaphas was undeterred, countering, "He stirs up the people all over Judea with his teaching. He started in Galilee and has come all the way here" (Lk. 23:5).

Recognizing an opportunity to deflect responsibility, Pilate asked if Jesus was indeed from Galilee.

Although unsure of Pilate's motive, Caiaphas confirmed it. Grateful for an out, Pilate informed Caiaphas that he had no jurisdiction over Jesus and would send him to Herod Antipas for evaluation, silently hoping Herod would handle the situation.

Conveniently, Herod Antipas was in Jerusalem for Passover. He always stayed in the city during major Jewish holidays to ensure everything ran smoothly, as the large gatherings increased the potential for disturbances.

Pilate had his guards and servant get Jesus. Then he told the servant to take Jesus to King Herod Antipas and relay the events of the previous night to him. He also reminded the servant to let Herod know that because Jesus was from Galilee, it was his responsibility, and the verdict was his to make. The walk to Herod's Jerusalem palace was less than a quarter of a mile.

While frustrated, Caiaphas and his crowd agreed to Pilate's decision and went along to hear what Jesus had to say to Herod

Antipas. Perhaps he would issue the order to kill Jesus. So, the group—Pilate's servant, the guards, Jesus, Caiaphas, and his whipped-up crowd—went to where Herod Antipas was staying in Jerusalem.

Herod Antipas was especially pleased to finally meet Jesus, as he had heard much about Jesus' healings and miracles. Now Herod hoped to see a miracle or some magic trick himself; perhaps he would be able to make Jesus an ally in helping him rule. To soften Jesus, he gave him a royal robe. Seeing the robe, Jesus stoically showed no emotion and did not reach to touch it.

Herod asked Jesus many questions, but Jesus never answered him. Instead, he stayed silent and stoic. While Herod asked his questions, Caiaphas and his crowd kept badgering Jesus and accusing him of being an inciter.

Seeing Jesus would not speak or accept the robe, Herod became irritated and began ridiculing him. Then others in Herod's court also joined in by mocking Jesus.

Frustrated, Herod said, "Dress him in the robe and send him back to Pilate." People in his entourage then dressed Jesus in the royal robe he had given him and began mocking Jesus for claiming to be a king. Still, Jesus did not respond.

Back to Pilate they went, with Jesus in tow. Caiaphas's patience was thinning, and anxiety mounted. Time was of the essence—the longer this dragged on, the higher the risk of Jesus' loyal followers causing a disturbance. Despite his growing anxiety, Caiaphas was careful to mask his nervousness.

Seeing the crowd and Jesus return, Pilate had hoped that Herod had settled the matter. However, he quickly realized that Herod had deferred the decision back to him. Disappointed and vexed, Pilate decided to make one more attempt to use reason to defuse this escalating situation. He beckoned Caiaphas and the other leaders to join him at the top of the steps. Once they had gathered, Pilate cast a resolute gaze over them and the crowd below. Then, raising his voice for all to hear, he began,

You brought me this man as one who was inciting the people to rebellion. I have examined him in your presence and have found no basis for your charges against him. Neither has Herod, for he sent him back to us; as you can see, he has done nothing to deserve death. Therefore, I will punish him and then release him. (Lk. 23:14–16)

This was not the outcome either the crowd or the leaders had hoped for. They vociferously rejected Pilate's decision.

Realizing he wasn't making headway in pacifying the crowd, Pilate took Jesus back into the courtyard for further questioning, but Jesus remained silent. In mounting desperation, Pilate sought a reason from Jesus to justify his release. Yet, Jesus offered no response. Pilate's frustration grew, but so did his admiration for Jesus' resilience.

Pilate couldn't fathom the calm demeanor Jesus maintained under the looming threat of execution. Neither the crowd's hostility nor the impending danger seemed to faze Jesus. He remained stoic throughout. Pilate, in need of a resolution, hoped that Herod might provide one. That hope, however, was dashed. And despite his probing, Jesus offered little to work with. Taking a moment to think, Pilate seated himself, pondering a solution to this intricate predicament.

A tradition then came to his mind: it was customary for him to release one prisoner during the Jewish festivals. Given that this was the time of the Festival of Unleavened Bread and the Passover, he thought he might be able to placate the crowd by offering to release a prisoner far more notorious than Jesus. He selected Barabbas, a well-known insurrectionist and murderer.

Rising from his seat, Pilate gestured for the guards to approach. In hushed tones, he instructed them to fetch Barabbas, and they should come back to the top of the courtyard steps.

Once the guards returned with a shackled Barabbas, Pilate posed a question to the crowd, "Do you want me to release to you

the king of the Jews or Barabbas?" (Mk. 15:9). Yet, Caiaphas manip-
ulated the crowd, urging them to opt for Barabbas's release (Mk.
15:11).

Hearing the crowd's preference and feeling cornered, Pilate
pressed the leaders and the crowd, "What shall I do, then, with the
one you call the king of the Jews?" (Mk. 15:12).

Unified in their thirst for retribution, the crowd fervently
chanted, "Crucify him!" (Mk. 15:13).

Pilate, seeking clarity, inquired, "Why? What crime has he committed?" (Mk. 15:14).

Their response, even more vehement, echoed back: "Crucify
him!" (Mk. 15:15).

At his wit's end, Pilate conceded to the crowd's wishes by re-
leasing Barabbas. However, he ordered that Jesus be flogged, hoping that this grave act might satiate the crowd's fury.

The Roman guards escorted Jesus to their headquarters. They
first removed the robe gifted to him by Herod. Leading him to an
outer courtyard, they fastened each of his hands to a post. Because
the post was low and the rope was short, Jesus was stooped over
with his back fully exposed.

Quickly, Caiaphas's crowd converged, forming a circle around
the courtyard. Their shouts of mockery echoed through the air as
they eagerly anticipated Jesus' demise.

Behind Jesus, a large muscular soldier picked up a whip, its
leather strips embedded with sharp metal pieces. He swung it over-
head, stretching his arm in preparation.

Suddenly, he lashed out, snapping the whip to accelerate it as
the leather strips embedded with metal dug into Jesus' back. The
studded whip left angry red marks on Jesus' flesh, which soon began
bleeding.

The executioner maintained a steady pace, striking Jesus repeatedly. With every hit, Jesus groaned, occasionally collapsing to his
knees, only to be lifted by the guards. His back became a brutal mo-
saic of wounds and blood. A particularly harsh strike landed on his

head, causing blood to pour over his face. Despite the agony, Jesus never cried out.

Over and over the whip cruelly met Jesus' back. Internally, Jesus knew this was part of the mission he was on. A mission of endurance and not punishment. While physically pained, Jesus stayed resolute.

Finally, remembering Pilate's directive to torture but not kill, the captain eventually called a halt to the proceedings, deeming any further punishment lethal.

Battered and bloody, Jesus was led back into the room, his robe thrown onto the floor. The soldiers dressed him in it, crafting a crown of thorns which they jammed onto his head. As they guided him towards Pilate, they jeered, "Hail, King of the Jews!"

Delivering the now haggard Jesus to Pilate, blood dripping and breaths labored, Pilate hoped the sight would deter the crowd's murderous intent. Emerging at the top of the steps, Pilate proclaimed to Caiaphas and the frenzied crowd, "Look, I am bringing him out to you to let you know that I find no basis for a charge against him" (Jn. 19:4). As Jesus, crowned with thorns and clad in the purple robe, appeared, Pilate announced, "Here is the man!" (Jn. 19:4–5).

However, Caiaphas and the mob were unwavering, demanding Jesus' crucifixion.

Distraught, Pilate retorted, "You take him and crucify him. As for me, I find no basis for a charge against him" (Jn. 19:6). Knowing Pilate's weak ploy, they countered, "Only you can condemn him"

Retreating to the palace with the barely mobile Jesus, a frustrated Pilate questioned him. Yet Jesus stayed mostly silent. Frustrated, Pilate said to Jesus, "Do you refuse to speak to me? Don't you realize I have power either to free you or to crucify you?"

Jesus then spoke and said, "You would have no power over me if it were not given to you from above. Therefore, the one who handed me over to you is guilty of a greater sin" (Jn. 19:11).

Reemerging, Pilate tried once more to sway the crowd. However, Caiaphas and the leaders threatened Pilate's allegiance to Caesar, further unnerving him.

Realizing his strategies were futile and fearing an uprising, Pilate washed his hands in a symbolic gesture, echoing Jesus' words, declaring, "I am innocent of this man's blood. It is your responsibility!" (Matt. 27:24).

The crowd's chilling response was unanimous: "His blood is on us and on our children!" (Matt. 27: 25).

Despite his reluctance, Pilate ultimately handed Jesus over for crucifixion (Jn. 19:16).

The Roman soldiers took Jesus away to the basement of Pilate's palace. The captain of the soldiers called together the whole company. The captain anticipated a potential revolt. By having all the soldiers present, he aimed to swiftly quell any opposition from the crowds.

Then they took off Jesus' robe, which Herod had given him, and replaced it with his original clothing. Once again, they forced the crown of thorns onto his head, causing Jesus more suffering.

Stooped over from the flogging and beatings, Jesus was led outside. Bloodied and exhausted, Jesus had great difficulty walking. Abruptly, they placed him before his cross. Jesus now knew it was inevitable, he was going to be crucified, yet he showed no fear.

In the first century, the cross was used by the Roman Empire as a symbol of humiliation. Jesus' cross was called a *low tau*.[36] In Greek, *tau* is the letter T. There were three types of crosses used for crucifixion. The first was called a *high tau,* where the crossbar was placed high on the opposing piece of wood. Jesus' cross or a *low tau,* allowing for a piece of wood to be placed just below the top. This piece usually carried a description of the person's crime. The third type of cross was a tree that was still alive in the ground, its branches used to nail an individual in place.

In 1870, Charles Rohault de Fleury estimated Jesus' cross weighed around 220 pounds.[37] It stood seven to nine feet tall, and the crossbar was five feet wide. Jesus would not have been able to carry the cross; instead, he would drag the cross. By dragging the cross, its effective weight would be reduced to 55 pounds.[38]

Already weakened, Jesus was commanded to shoulder his cross and commence the journey to Calvary, also known as Golgotha in Aramaic.

Calvary, located outside the city's northwest walls, was the Romans' chosen site for crucifixions, a mere 2,000-foot trek from Pilate's palace. Today, this route, dotted with 14 stations, takes believers through bustling Jerusalem streets, retracing Jesus' path, now named the Way of Suffering, or Via Delarosa.

Crucifying individuals at the city's outskirts was a strategic Roman practice, sending a stern message to those entering. This day, the grim spectacle would be amplified as Jesus and two criminals would be raised on crosses, visible to all.

Jesus, with great difficulty, managed to lift and rest the cross on his shoulder. But as he trudged on, his strength waned. Recognizing he couldn't bear the cross alone, the soldiers singled out a stout and strong bystander named Simon from Cyrene and forced him to assist Jesus.

Interestingly, Simon's town, Cyrene, was in modern-day Libya. It is now an archeological site near the village of Shahhat. In the first century, Cyrene held close to 100,000 Jews whose ancestors had settled in the area around 300 BC. They also had a synagogue they used in Jerusalem, as many would make the trek to celebrate the holidays.[39]

Besides his appearance of great strength, when the Roman soldiers had eyed Simon's attire, they deduced he wasn't of the local Hebrew populace. Assuming he wasn't Jewish and, therefore, less likely to resist, they selected him. But they were mistaken. Simon was indeed Jewish and had journeyed over a thousand miles to attend the holy festivities in Jerusalem.

Together, amidst the dusty road and looming dread, Jesus and Simon trudged on, the crossbar weighing heavy on their shoulders. Moments came when Jesus, drained, would falter, but Simon, seemingly with supernatural strength, would lift Jesus with one arm, all the while balancing the cross's weight with his other.

The distance they had to drag the roughly 220 lb. cross was made harder by the incline to Calvary. As word had gotten out about Jesus being sentenced, slowly, many of his followers and other onlookers started to line the way to Calvary.

When Jesus arrived outside of Calvary, he and Simon dropped the cross to the ground. Then, he was stripped of his outer garments while soldiers threw dice to see who would get them. A soldier filled with compassion attempted to give Jesus wine and myrrh to dull his pain. But Jesus refused.

The guards placed Jesus face up on top of the cross with his hands and feet tied to the cross so they would not move when the nails were hammered into his hands and feet.

Cruelly, the guards began pounding nails into Jesus' hands and ankles. First, they nailed his hands; with a single stroke, a nail pierced his left hand, causing Jesus to visibly shake with pain. Then, another nail was driven through his right hand, making Jesus shudder again. Finally, the guards began hammering a long spike through his crossed ankles. It took several painful blows to secure. With each strike, Jesus winced.

As the guards were nailing Jesus to the cross, he uttered, "Father, forgive them, for they do not know what they are doing," a remarkable statement of compassion and forgiveness during the most difficult and painful moment of Jesus' earthly life.

The guards lifted Jesus and the cross up. Next, the group of soldiers placed it into a hole they had dug for support. As Jesus was lifted up, his body sagged forward pressing in on his lungs, which made his breathing more belabored. Many who were crucified would eventually suffocate because of the weight of their bodies.

On the piece of wood on top of his cross, Pilate had the soldiers write the inscription THE KING OF THE JEWS. The leaders and Caiaphas had vehemently argued against this, but Pilate had refused to change his mind.

It was now mid-morning. People loyal to Caiaphas who walked by hurled insults at Jesus, some saying, "So! You who are going to destroy the temple and build it in three days, come down from the cross and save yourself!" (Mk. 15:29–30).

Next to Jesus were two other crosses with criminals also being crucified, one on the left of Jesus, the other on the right. The criminal on the left mocked and spat at Jesus. At one point he said, "Aren't you the Messiah? Save yourself and us!" (Lk. 23:39).

The criminal on the right, irritated by his compatriot's comments, immediately rebuked him.

> "Don't you fear God," he said, "since you are under the same sentence? We are punished justly, for we are getting what our deeds deserve. But this man has done nothing wrong." (Lk. 23:40–41)

Then the criminal said, "Jesus, remember me when you come into your kingdom" (Lk. 23:42).

Although he was suffering and barely alive, Jesus answered him, "Truly I tell you, today you will be with me in paradise" (Lk. 23:43).

An eerie gloom fell over the area and the bystanders. As the hours went by, Jesus' breath became more and more labored. Beyond his severe physical pain, Jesus began to feel the indescribably intense pain of all of humankind's sins being borne by him. Sins of a mundane nature and sins of great depravity became Jesus' to absorb. Jesus was now the sacrificial lamb, absorbing all of humankind's sin.

Finally, in his full humanity, Jesus cried out, "My God, my God, why have you forsaken me?" (Mk. 15:34).

Those who were standing near heard this and said, "Listen, he is calling Elijah" (Mk. 15:35). Those standing by missed that Jesus wasn't crying out to the prophet Elijah, but Eloi. Eloi is another expression of God and literally means, in Hebrew, "God of me." An awful darkness fell over the area as Jesus hung, suffering.

Jesus' human body was shutting down. He was suffocating and quickly losing body fluids. Each of his major organs was failing. His heart and lungs were stiffening from the loss of blood. His human end was near.

It was now mid-afternoon; knowing this, the soldiers did not want to leave Jesus on the cross with the approaching Sabbath. They discussed breaking his legs to hasten his death. As they were discussing this, Jesus said, "It is finished" (Jn. 19:30). Then, he released one last groan and his human form died.

When Jesus said, "It is finished," he was declaring he had completed God's will. His physical pain and the absorption of all human sin was over. He had finished the brutal part of redemption. Now only his wonderous divinity was left. He had come to serve humanity as human and had finished his difficult task.

At the same time, the curtain in the temple was torn in two. A Roman soldier who stood nearby and watched the whole crucifixion said, "Surely this man was the Son of God!" (Mk. 15:39).

The tearing of the curtain, which separated the sacred temple room of the Holy of Holies, was symbolic of the new life Jesus had just created for the world. No longer was the temple in Jerusalem the way to God. But through faith in the blood Jesus had shed for humankind, all people could find God. Essentially, God had moved from the temple.

One of the soldiers took a spear and pierced Jesus' side to confirm his death. The earthly body of Jesus stayed limp—his suffering was over.

Upon seeing this, Jesus' mother, Mary, and the other women of his ministry began to weep. A rich man named Joseph of Arimathea was standing nearby and was greatly moved. He had really never agreed with Caiaphas's course of action against Jesus. But now, after witnessing Jesus' death, he was overcome with emotion and was sure Jesus was who he said he was.

Likewise, Nicodemus was also in attendance. After wondering where he should place his loyalty—Jesus or a comfortable life—he now knew Jesus was where his heart belonged. Both men had stood quietly in the crowd as Jesus suffered. At times, they had looked at each other and winced as Jesus was tortured and put on the cross. Now, uncaring about the consequences of their support for Jesus, the two went over to each other to share silently in their dismay.

Seeing Jesus had died and desiring to get the body buried before the start of the Sabbath, Nicodemus and Joseph of Arimathea went to Pilate to lay claim to Jesus' body. Before they left, they asked the guards to stand by the body and told them they were going to Pilate to request permission to have Jesus' body.

When Pilate heard from Joseph of Arimathea and Nicodemus that Jesus had died, he was surprised he had died so quickly. To ensure he wasn't being tricked, he asked for a centurion to come tell him if Jesus had really died. When the centurion arrived and confirmed Jesus' death, Pilate allowed them to have the body.

Interestingly, a non-biblical document exists that is attributed to Nicodemus, describing Jesus' trial and crucifixion. The document's account is similar to those from the four gospels and is called the Gospel of Nicodemus. The earliest surviving scraps of this writing are from the fourth or fifth century.[40]

On their way back to Calvary to retrieve Jesus' body, Joseph bought a linen cloth and Nicodemus bought the spices for his burial. When they arrived at the cross, they found Jesus and the cross lying on the ground. The guards stood solemnly, protecting Jesus' body.

The two men with the help of the guards extracted the nails from his hands and ankles. Then, Joseph of Arimathea and Nicodemus took Jesus' body and wrapped it in the linen cloth. Inside the cloth, they had spread the spices. They and the guards carried the body to a nearby tomb cut out of rock in a nearby garden. Interestingly, no one had been buried in this garden at this point. Today, the Church of the Holy Sepulchre stands on this spot.

Joseph of Arimathea and Nicodemus placed Jesus on a rock slab and said a prayer. Then, together with the guards, they rolled a stone to cover the opening of the grave.

The suddenness of Jesus' death seemed surreal. Just days ago, he had been celebrated by many.

8

HOLY SATURDAY—A "HARROWING HELL"

Nissan 16 (Saturday, April 4, AD 33)

THE DAY AFTER JESUS' DEATH, CAIAPHAS RETURNED TO the temple. He believed he had dealt with the challenge posed by Jesus, yet a lingering doubt remained. The more he tried to assure himself it was over, the more unease settled in.

What gnawed at him was the circulating claim that Jesus had proclaimed, "They will kill him, and on the third day he will rise again" (Matt. 17:23). Though Caiaphas viewed this with skepticism, he recognized that Jesus' disciples might not. Drawing together a council of priests and Pharisee leaders, he voiced his concerns, highlighting Jesus' prediction. He expressed his apprehension that Jesus followers might attempt to take the body, asserting a miraculous resurrection.

After some discussion, they went to Pilate to demand a guard be placed at Jesus' tomb. Annoyed, Pilate met with the group, hoping the previous day would have ended the Jesus drama. But here they were back again.

Caiaphas and his fellow priests said to Pilate,

> Sir, ... we remember that while he was still alive that de-
> ceiver said, "After three days I will rise again." So, give
> the order for the tomb to be made secure until the third
> day. Otherwise, his disciples may come and steal the
> body and tell the people that he has been raised from the
> dead. This last deception will be worse than the first.
> (Matt. 27:63–64)

Hoping this would end the issue, Pilate agreed and gave the group soldiers to guard the tomb. The group—Caiaphas, the priests, and the soldiers—went to the tomb and found a large stone was already sealing the opening. The guards were posted to watch and ensure no one came to roll back the stone and steal the body.

Judas Repents

That same Friday, Judas had witnessed both trials, the first with Caiaphas and his thugs, the second in front of Pilate. At each trial, Judas grew more remorseful of his actions. When he had taken the 30 coins from the priests to betray Jesus, it was in a petulant fit of anger and greed. As he watched Jesus get beaten and the trials unfold, he realized just what he had done.

Despite his mental attempts to dismiss his feelings of remorse, they only grew deeper. The remorse slowly took hold of his being until it was too large. When the remorse was firmly entrenched, Judas sank into a deep, mental abyss. Like all sin, the calamity was not revealed until it was too late.

As Jesus was led away to be crucified, bloodied and weak, Judas' error fully descended upon him. Realizing the gravity of his actions, Judas went back to the priests. He stormed into the temple and threw the 30 pieces of silver onto the floor. Then he said to the priests, "I have sinned, for I have betrayed innocent blood" (Matt. 27:4).

Upon seeing this, the priests, desiring to distance themselves from the act of betrayal, replied, "What is that to us? That's your responsibility" (Matt. 27:4).

Judas left the priests and began a difficult walk alone. The thought of Jesus being tortured because of him was unbearable. How he longed to change the past!

Seeing the money on the floor, the priests gathered it up. After a brief discussion, they concluded that it couldn't be put back in the temple treasury, as it was blood money. So they decided to use the money to buy a potter's field as a burial place for foreigners and the poor. With this purchase, what was spoken by Jeremiah the prophet was fulfilled.

Centuries earlier, the great prophet Jeremiah had foretold Judas' betrayal. This is another harkening message for humankind from the ancient prophets who foretold the arrival and life events of Jesus:

> Then that which was spoken through Jeremiah the prophet was fulfilled, saying, They took the thirty pieces of silver, the price set on him by the people of Israel, and they used them to buy the potter's field, as the Lord commanded me. (Matt. 27:9–10)

After his remorseful visit to the priests to give back the silver coins, Judas went out into the streets of Jerusalem. He wandered aimlessly through the city, hoping it would soothe him. Finally, he found a place to sit. As he sat, his mind vacillated between rationalizing his behavior and being overcome by a deep sense of remorse. He struggled to explain to himself why he had allowed evil to enter his being and make an innocent Jesus suffer. He had loved Jesus and only now understood he acted out of selfish impulse.

A seemingly cosmic (spiritual) battle was raging within him. One moment he felt he could soothe himself; the next he was overwhelmed by immense feelings of despair. Unable to resolve this internal conflict, he stood up and began walking again.

Throughout the day and long night, he repeated these efforts, but as soon as he found relief, it would disappear. Finally, Judas went outside the city. As he walked, he found and picked up some rope.

As Jesus had said during the last supper, "The Son of Man will go just as it is written about him. But woe to that man who betrays the Son of Man! It would be better for him if he had not been born" (Matt. 26:24). In that moment of great despair, that was how Judas felt.

With each hour that passed, his despair became insurmountable. Then, seeing a tree, he went to its base. The single lone tree would be his answer. He tied the rope around his neck and strategically looped it around a branch. Lifting himself up into a notch high up in the tree, he paused for a moment and issued a final cry. Then, he jumped, and the rope tightened.

He hung there for days. Those who passed by ignored what they saw. Finally, the rope gave out and his bloated body fell onto the ground. After hitting the ground, his lifeless body exploded with blood pouring out.

Coincidently, the land he fell on was the plot the priests had bought with the blood money they had paid him. As a result, this place would become known as the *Field of Blood*.

A Scene of Despair

On the night Jesus was arrested, all of the disciples but Peter had fled. Peter had followed Jesus and those who arrested him into Jerusalem. The other 10 later met up at the house where they had been staying. Fearful of being arrested as well, they sat in the house, discussing where they could go to protect themselves. After much discussion, they agreed to stay in Bethany. Staying in Bethany in a locked house would provide them some protection from others.

Additionally, fleeing from Jerusalem during the holy period of Passover and the Sabbath would have made the apostles stand out, making it easier to be found and become arrested. There was also the issue of staying close to the women, who had stayed in the area to anoint Jesus' body. After all these considerations, the apostles agreed it would be wise to stay concealed in Bethany.

Peter was despondent and couldn't shake the feeling that he hadn't done enough to support and protect Jesus. Instead of standing by Jesus, he had constantly denied him. During the day, he wandered Jerusalem in a state of hopelessness. Any attempt on his part to understand why he hadn't been more loyal was met with horror in his mind.

He tried to calm himself, but each attempt was met with a gasp of disbelief at what he had done. With nowhere else to turn, he sought the company of the other apostles, hoping to find them in Bethany. Despondent, he walked back to their previous lodging near the Mount of Olives. When he arrived at the house they stayed in, he was relieved to have found the others.

The women who had gone to Jesus's crucifixion were there as well. They busied themselves with preparations for going to Jesus' tomb after the Sabbath.

A Harrowing Hell

Over the centuries, many have wondered and asked, "Where was Jesus on Saturday, after the crucifixion?" We find a clue in the often-recited Christian credo called the Apostles' Creed. In the first section, it says about Jesus, "he descended into hell, rose again from the dead on the third day."

This creed originated in the fourth or fifth century. It was developed by early Christian leaders, and parts of it are found in letters or documents written by early church theologians, like Augustine, Tertullian, Ambrose, and Irenaeus. More importantly, the Apostles' Creed's inclusion echoes Ephesians 4:9, where it says, "What does 'he ascended' mean except that he also descended to the lower, earthly regions?"

The term, "Harrowing Hell," first appears in the *Gospel of Nicodemus* under the section titled Acts of Pilate. It also appears in another document titled the *Acts of Peter and Paul* which is attributed to the fifth century.[41] Based on the verse in Ephesians, it appears Jesus descended into the *lowly earth regions* or the "Harrowing Hell." So what did Jesus do while in the *lowly earth regions*?

First Peter 3:18-19 states, "For Christ also suffered once for sins, the righteous for the unrighteous, to bring you to God. He was put to death in the body but made alive in the Spirit. After being made alive, he went and made proclamation to the imprisoned spirits." From this verse, we can interpret that Jesus preached the good news of salvation in the "Harrowing Hell."

Later in 1 Peter 4:6 it says, "For this is the reason the gospel was preached even to those who are now dead..." Again suggesting Jesus preached to the dead.

We should also understand the purpose of Jesus' descent into the "Harrowing Hell." Colossians 1:18 provides insight, stating: "And he is the head of the body, the church; he is the beginning and the firstborn from among the dead, so that in everything he might have supremacy." For those who had died, both in the past and in the future, to be saved, Jesus had to be the first to rise.

In understanding this information, we can know that Jesus, while physically dead, remained alive in spirit—his divinity intact. In this state, He proclaimed the good news to the souls of the deceased. As the "Alpha and Omega," he was the first to rise from the dead, setting a precedent for all who follow Him.

The souls of those who died before Jesus' time had the opportunity to hear his message during his descent. For people living from Jesus' time until now, as well as those in the future, salvation comes through faith in the risen Jesus.

This faith connects believers across time—from the era before Christ through his life and resurrection and into the present and future—uniting them in the salvation made possible through Jesus Christ.

The definition of "harrowing" also gives us another clue about Jesus' activity.

In the Merriam-Webster Dictionary, "harrowing" means "acutely distressing or painful." However, in Old English, we find an additional meaning: "to break the ground in preparation for planting." In other words, harrowing means "preparing all souls who believe for eternal life."

So what did Jesus do on Saturday? He prepared to become the first to lead others to eternal life. He preached to souls gone before him. And, like Jonah, he escaped from the beast on the third day.

Jesus "The Word" Lives On

Jesus died fully human but lived on as fully divine. In our human understanding, this concept can be hard to comprehend. Only through faith can it truly be understood and believed. Part of moving toward knowing who Jesus is in a divine sense requires being fully committed to believing that the words of the Bible are inspired by God. In John 1:1, we get help in understanding his divinity.

Previously, we analyzed the verse John 1:1 where Jesus' status was explained as being with God and being God. It also explained Jesus was with and was God from the beginning. This is a start to understanding Jesus' divinity.

As a reminder, if we rewrite John 1:1 using Jesus' name instead of the word "Word," the meaning becomes clearer. Then, it would say, "In the beginning was Jesus, and Jesus was with God, and Jesus was God." In other words, Jesus existed at the beginning, was with God from the start, and is God.

Stopping here and meditating on Jesus as being with God and being God is fundamental to knowing Jesus is divine. Here is where God-given inspiration and personal experiences with God and Jesus help us accept this as true.

Another verse later in John may also help us to understand Jesus' divinity and humanity more fully: "The Word became flesh and made his dwelling among us. We have seen his glory, the glory of the one and only Son, who came from the Father, full of grace and truth" (Jn. 1:14). Once again, if we substitute the word "*Word*" with Jesus, we see "Jesus became flesh." Flesh refers to his humanity.

So, Jesus arrived on earth fully human and fully divine, meaning Jesus had all the *human* characteristics and, at the same time, was *divine*. In Jesus' humanness, we can understand his anxiety in Gethsemane and his pain on the cross—the pain which became almost overwhelming as he accepted all human sin and died as a human.

Jesus' incarnation as a human was pivotal to the grand design of salvation. By becoming fully man while retaining his divinity, Jesus embodied the essence of humanity, complete with its vulnerabilities, emotions, and temptations.

His sacrificial death and triumphant resurrection were not just symbolic acts; they were the foundational events that paved the way for humanity's redemption. In rising from the dead, Jesus became the first fruits of the resurrection, establishing a precedent for all of humanity.

Those who have passed before and those yet to come can find hope in the promise of eternal life, following the path Jesus forged. His human journey and victorious resurrection affirm that death is not the end but a doorway to a new beginning for all who believe in him.

Jesus needed to die as a human to serve as our intermediary with God. Through his sacrificial death, he absorbed all sin. It is through Jesus that we forge an eternal bond with God. This is why we conclude our prayers with, "In Jesus' name."

He died much like the sacrificial lamb of Passover. his blood, like the lamb's blood of the first Passover, protects those who believe.

At the Passover supper on Thursday night, we get more insight into Jesus' divine nature. Phillip asked Jesus, "Lord, show us the Father and that will be enough for us" (Jn. 14:8).

Jesus replied,

> Have I been with you so long, and still you do not know me, Phillip? Whoever has seen me has seen the Father.

How can you say, "Show us the Father"? Do you not believe that I am in the Father and the Father is in me? The words that I say to you I do not speak on my own authority, but the Father who dwells in me does his works. Believe me that I am in the Father and the Father is in me, or else believe in the works themselves. (Jn. 14:9–11 ESV)

It is clear from this statement the relationship Jesus has with God is so close, they are of one mind. As bystanders seeing or hearing this conversation, we can wonder why Phillip didn't simply believe. But when we consider our own lives, can't we relate? From a human standpoint, nothing in our human experience can logically explain Jesus and the relationship he has with God. But when we apply our own personal relationship with Jesus and have faith, the concept is far easier to understand. And that is Jesus' point to Phillip.

Jesus was with God but also is God. When he arrived on earth, Jesus took on the characteristics of being human as well. While we can't physically do this ourselves, it doesn't mean Jesus can't.

Another interesting aspect of the statement from John 14:9–11 is Jesus using the phrase "I AM" in the last sentence. Once again, if we go back to Exodus 3:14 where we read in all capital letters "I AM WHO I AM," we see this was God's reply to Moses when Moses first asked God how he should refer to him if others asked. Jesus is saying the same thing.

Again, faith is important to help us understand. Faith that the Bible is holy and inspired by God is critical to our understanding of Jesus. Human logic and reasoning will not get us over this hurdle, but faith will.

The more we practice our faith, the more we see the truth of the Bible, which in turn creates a stronger faith in us. Also, as we pray and receive answers, we see Jesus working in our lives, which in turn provides us with a stronger faith. Leading us to firmly know Jesus is part of the Holy Trinity, or Godhead—three forms in one: God, Son (Jesus), and the Holy Spirit.

On Holy Saturday, Jesus was liberating souls, leading and emancipating them from the depths of the tormenting abyss. known as the "Harrowing Hell."

9

HE IS RISEN

Nissan 17 (Sunday, April 5, AD 33)

EARLY SUNDAY MORNING, MARY MAGDALENE, MARY the mother of James, and Salome went to Jesus' tomb. They brought spices to anoint Jesus' body, unaware that Joseph of Arimathea and Nicodemus had already completed this task. As they walked, the sun began to crest over the horizon, casting a bright yellow glow that outlined the hills. The women moved closer to the tomb, speaking little and deeply focused on their solemn act of devotion.

Suddenly, the ground shook with a great earthquake. An angel descended from heaven and approached Jesus' tomb. The guards stationed there, overcome with fear, fled. The angel then rolled back the stone and sat on it.

Feeling the quake, the women were initially stunned. They hesitated and took a seat on a nearby rock, waiting to see if there would be further tremors. After a few moments of calm, they continued on their way.

As they ascended the hill, Mary Magdalene recalled that a stone had been placed in front of the tomb and that she'd heard it was being guarded by soldiers. She turned to Mary and Salome, voicing her concerns about rolling the stone away and whether the soldiers would even allow them access. They discussed it among themselves, uncertain of the outcome. Despite their lingering unease from the earthquake, they remained steadfast in their goal—to prepare Jesus' body.

Jesus had been hastily entombed late Friday afternoon, right before sundown—the beginning of the Sabbath. Custom dictated that no work could be performed on the Sabbath, certainly not the preparation of a body for burial. Joseph of Arimathea and Nicodemus had just enough time to anoint Jesus' body with spices.

These spices served a dual purpose. Primarily, they masked the odor of decomposition, as embalming wasn't the practice in ancient Jerusalem. Additionally, they formally anointed the body—a gesture of deep love and devotion in those times.

Rounding a bend in the path, the tomb came into sight. To their astonishment, no guards were present, and the stone was already rolled away. With a mix of bewilderment and urgency, they entered the tomb. Inside, they found a young man seated on the right side, dressed in a white robe, but Jesus' body was absent. Distressed, they all exclaimed, "Where is Jesus?"

The young man answered,

> Don't be alarmed …. You are looking for Jesus the Nazarene, who was crucified. He has risen! He is not here. See the place where they laid him. (Mk. 16:6)

The three women fled the tomb, both perplexed and frightened. They had yet to grasp the implications of the vacant tomb.

After covering a short distance, Mary Magdalene paused to collect her thoughts. She instructed the other two to return to the house in Bethany and inform the rest of what they had witnessed. She decided to head back to the tomb to see if any others from their group were coming.

As Mary retraced her steps to the tomb, she spotted two figures in the distance, down in the valley. Quickening her pace, she approached them. As she neared, she recognized them as Peter and Thomas.

Once she was within earshot, she called out, "Peter! Thomas!"

Hearing their names, Peter and Thomas turned to find Mary Magdalene approaching. They could see the distress on her face. When she reached them, she blurted out, "They have taken the Lord out of the tomb, and we don't know where they've placed Him" (Jn. 20:2).

Quickly, both Peter and Thomas went up the hill toward the tomb. Thomas, swifter of foot, reached the entrance first. He paused, peering inside, and saw the linen shroud that Joseph of Arimathea had procured to wrap Jesus. It lay discarded.

Following closely behind, Peter went directly into the tomb. He observed not only the linen wrap but also the separate cloth that had covered Jesus' face. It was set aside, neatly folded. This detail struck Peter; had thieves taken Jesus' body, they wouldn't have taken the time to fold the cloth.

Though both Peter and Thomas had listened to Jesus' predictions of His resurrection, the full meaning had eluded them. But now, with the Spirit stirring within him, the sight of the empty tomb, the displaced stone, and the meticulously folded facecloth resonated with Peter. He understood—Jesus had risen. Thomas, however, remained skeptical.

Amazed, both men realized they needed to inform the others, and they hurried back to Bethany to share the startling news.

The guards, who had fled following the earthquake, headed straight to the priests in Jerusalem to recount the events at the tomb. A group convened rapidly to discuss this unprecedented turn of events.

Upon Caiaphas's arrival, he was filled with apprehension, wondering when the issue with Jesus would finally end! The group deliberated among themselves. Eventually, Caiaphas instructed them to bribe the soldiers. Handing over the money, they told the guards, "You are to say, 'His disciples came during the night and stole him away while we were asleep.' If this report reaches the governor, we will appease him and ensure you face no repercussions" (Matt. 28:13-14).

Mary Magdalene Sees Jesus

Mary Magdalene was consumed by sadness. After Peter and Thomas left, she sat on a rock away from the tomb. The trauma of seeing Jesus die coupled with the uncertainty of where his body was consumed her thoughts. Remaining there on that rock was no comfort to her. Moved by the Spirit, she decided to return to the empty tomb.

Upon reaching the tomb, she once again tried to calm her swirling emotions and found another rock to sit upon. No amount of reasoning could comfort her, so she remained by the tomb, crying deeply.

Her grief was intense. Initially, it was a feeling of disbelief from the events of Friday. Over the subsequent days, the grief grew. Now, in this lonely spot, the stark reality was almost too much. Yet, she felt drawn back to the tomb.

Standing up, she approached the tomb's entrance. Stooping to look inside, she was taken aback to see two angels. "Woman, why are you weeping?" they asked (Jn. 20:13).

Looking up, she replied, "They have taken away my Lord, and I do not know where they have laid him" (Jn. 20:14).

Feeling a presence behind her, she turned but did not recognize Jesus. He asked, "Woman, why are you weeping? Whom are you seeking?" (Jn. 20:15).

Thinking he was the gardener, she pleaded, "Sir, if you have carried him away, tell me where you have laid him, and I will take him away" (Jn. 20:15).

Then he simply said, "Mary."

She then realized it was Jesus. Overwhelmed, she exclaimed, "Rabboni!" which means "teacher."

Jesus told her, "Do not cling to me, for I have not yet ascended to the Father. Go to my brothers and say to them, 'I am ascending to my Father and your Father, to my God and your God'" (Jn. 20:16–17).

Her grief vanished, replaced by profound relief. Her tears of sorrow transformed into tears of joy. She had seen Jesus—alive! She rushed to the house in Bethany where the disciples stayed.

Bursting through the door and out of breath, she exclaimed, "I have seen the Lord!" (Jn. 20:18). Her palpable excitement began to instill hope in those present.

The apostles, except for Thomas, were there. Peter, Mary the mother of James, and Salome, having visited the empty tomb earlier, had shared their experiences. Some wondered if it was their imagination, while others held onto hope. They were puzzled: why hadn't Jesus appeared to them if he was alive? Their time together during Jesus' ministry made his absence even more perplexing. Additionally, they were wary of Caiaphas or the Roman authorities trying to trap them.

However, with Mary Magdalene's firsthand account of meeting Jesus, their fear began to wane, replaced by hope. Their original plan to leave for Galilee was now in question as they eagerly discussed their next steps.

Thomas Declares Himself Impure

Thomas, ever pragmatic, had accompanied Peter to the tomb to better understand the events. Upon arrival, he noticed the stone had been removed, allowing for an easy peek inside, which he took advantage of. After Peter entered, Thomas did the same.

Being a strict follower of customs and tradition, Thomas had hesitated about entering the tomb. He knew that by Jewish tradition, doing so could render him impure. After venturing inside, he pondered whether he needed to observe a period of isolation.

On their return, he expressed his concerns about impurity to Peter. Peter, having listened, reassured Thomas that since the body wasn't there, he needn't worry. Nevertheless, Thomas remained conflicted.

His initial decision to enter the tomb had been driven by curiosity. True, the body wasn't there when he looked, but it had been at some point. Engulfed in internal debate, he finally resolved to observe a seven-day period of isolation, abiding by the customs and traditions pertaining to impurity.

Informing Peter of his decision, he took leave. He found an abandoned dwelling not far from where the other disciples and the women were lodging. But before settling in for his prescribed seven days, he visited the others.

Upon knocking, he stepped back, awaiting an answer. When the door opened, Peter, curious about the distance Thomas kept, inquired about his aloofness. Thomas explained his concerns regarding impurity and informed Peter of his temporary dwelling. He requested Peter to keep him updated on any new developments.

Thomas, always pragmatic and compassionate, wanted to ensure his potential impurity didn't impact others. He reiterated to Peter that he would be in isolation for seven days. While Peter didn't 'necessarily agree, he refrained from argument, appreciating Thomas's transparency.

At this juncture, it's important to delve into the identity of Thomas. John 20:2 refers to "the other disciple" who went into the tomb. Later in John 20:3, this disciple is termed "the one Jesus loved." So, who exactly is this disciple? The surrounding circumstances suggest it was Thomas.

Tradition proposes it was John, the author of the Gospel of John. However, scholars contest this claim. In reality, there's no concrete evidence supporting this tradition.

Some scholars will still say it wasn't Thomas. But others, supported by extensive research, will say the *other disciple* is Thomas, notably a scholar named, James Charlesworth.[42]

Here's a key argument, shared by myself and others, advocating for Thomas as the "other disciple:" Thomas did not witness the resurrected Jesus until eight days later. To vanish from one's companions after enduring the trauma of Jesus' crucifixion seems illogical. However, if Thomas was indeed the other disciple who entered the empty tomb, this behavior aligns perfectly. First-century Jews who strictly adhered to purity rules would know to separate themselves upon entering a tomb containing a body. Given that Thomas was absent for seven days and would encounter Jesus on the eighth day, it's a logical inference that he was the other disciple.

Earlier, Thomas stood out as the lone member of the Twelve who supported Jesus' decision to return to Jerusalem. He demonstrated an unyielding loyalty to Jesus, unafraid of the potentially fatal consequences.

Answering the question: Who was the "other disciple?" The answer appears to be Thomas. While this interpretation might not be widely recognized, the evidence strongly suggests Thomas was the "other disciple."

Jesus Visits the Apostles and Women

Around dusk, even though the doors were locked, Jesus appeared to those in the house. He said, "Peace be with you" (Jn 20:19).

The occupants looked at each other, standing in awe and motionless. Observing their disbelief, Jesus showed them the wounds in his hands, his ankles, and his side where he had been pierced.

Upon seeing this, all were filled with amazement and their doubts dissolved. Some knelt in reverence, while others wept. It became clear to them that everything was true.

Many times, Jesus had foretold that he would die and then rise on the third day. Those who had been with him hadn't truly grasped the significance of this statement. Some thought it was merely metaphorical. But now, its meaning was clear.

Then Jesus addressed the group, "Peace be with you! As the Father has sent me, I am sending you." With these words, he breathed on them and declared, "Receive the Holy Spirit. If you forgive anyone's sins, their sins are forgiven; if you do not forgive them, they are not forgiven" (Jn. 20:21–23).

Almost immediately, the group felt the Spirit enter them. Their understanding deepened, and the purpose of the crucifixion became clear. They transitioned from mere human understanding to a divine realization.

Jesus had triumphed over death and was resurrected on the third day!

EPILOGUE

AFTER JESUS WAS CRUCIFIED AND ROSE ON THE THIRD day, the cross transformed from a symbol of brutal execution to one of hope and salvation for countless believers. What the Romans utilized to instill fear and exhibit their power has, in a twist of fate, become a beacon of hope for over two billion faithful individuals worldwide.

During Jesus' time on earth, he fulfilled his divine mission. He shared the good news with all who would listen, healed the ailing, restored sight to the blind, and shared meals with those society deemed unworthy. His greatest achievement was rising from the dead, signifying humanity's release from the shackles of sin. That pivotal Easter morning illuminated the route to redemption—through faith, we are now reconciled with God and saved.

Jesus' final hours were filled with unimaginable suffering. He faced brutal beatings and was crucified, enduring these agonies to bear the weight of humanity's sins, from the gravest to the most trivial. Through this profound act of love and obedience, Jesus paved the way for us to reunite with God. In his sacrifice, he established a new covenant between God and humanity.

After his resurrection, Jesus remained on earth for 40 more days, serving as living proof of his monumental miracle. During this period, he made numerous appearances, offering guidance and reassurance not just to his apostles but to many who had placed their faith in him.

In 1 Corinthians 15:3–8, the Apostle Paul notes that over 500 individuals witnessed Jesus during the 40 days following His resurrection. Intriguingly, Paul wrote this account around AD 50, a period when a significant number of these 500 witnesses would likely have still been alive. Notably, there is no documented contradiction to this account from those who had personal encounters with Jesus.

Thomas Is Convinced

After Jesus visited the men and women in Bethany on Easter Sunday, a group of apostles rushed to inform Thomas that they had encountered the Lord. Bursting with excitement, they located Thomas, who had isolated himself, and shared the news of Jesus' appearance. However, in line with his pragmatic disposition, Thomas responded,

> Unless I see the nail marks in his hands and put my finger where the nails were, and put my hand into his side, I will not believe. (Jn. 20:25)

A week later, Thomas ended his period of isolation. On the eighth day, feeling purified, he set out to reunite with the others. As he stepped into the house, the apostles, brimming with joy, eagerly recounted Jesus' miraculous visit.

As they conversed behind locked doors, Jesus appeared among them once more, offering, "Peace be with you!" (Jn. 20:26). Recognizing Thomas's need for tangible proof, Jesus turned to him, beckoning, "Put your finger here; see my hands. Reach out your hand and put it into my side. Stop doubting and believe." (Jn. 20:27)

In a stirring moment of revelation, Thomas fell to his knees, exclaiming, "My Lord and my God!" (Jn. 20:28). The sight of Jesus filled him with profound relief and elation. He not only realized that everything would be alright but also acknowledged the divine presence before him. The peace enveloping him was so profound that he struggled to hold back tears of joy.

Jesus then told him,

> Because you have seen me, you have believed; blessed are those who have not seen and yet have believed. (Jn. 20:29)

It wasn't that Thomas doubted; his practical mindset simply craved tangible proof. But Jesus reminded him that authentic faith transcends hard evidence and embraces the unseen. Through this encounter, Thomas understood that recognizing Jesus as God was more about spiritual faith than physical validation.

Like many of us, even though Thomas had yearned to accept Jesus as the Messiah, his analytical nature sought clarity and undeniable proof. While Jesus had provided that physical affirmation, he also emphasized the importance of faith.

Transformed by this event and Jesus, Thomas became a fervent missionary. As per tradition, he journeyed to India, establishing seven churches and preached until July 3, AD 72. On that fateful day, he met his end by a spear's thrust. Like most of his fellow apostles, his life ended with martyrdom.

Peter Accepts His Role

After convincing Thomas, Jesus wasn't quite finished teaching his apostles. At another visit by Jesus, he pulled Peter aside to talk with him. They had just finished eating breakfast, and Jesus said to Peter, "Simon, Son of John, do you love me more than these?" (Jn. 21:15). Curiously, Jesus used Simon's birth name here. Early in his ministry while he was gathering apostles, Jesus had changed Simon's name to Peter. Peter is Greek, and translated into English, it means "the rock." Calling Peter "Simon" was Jesus trying to remind him of who he was and who he wanted Peter to become—*the Rock.*

Just prior to this breakfast, Peter and six of the other apostles had gone fishing at night. Despite having labored all night, by dawn they had not caught any fish. As they were rowing to shore disappointed, Jesus appeared on the shore and told them to cast their net on the right side of the boat. When they did so, the net filled up with

153 large fish; it almost swamped the boat. All were stunned by this miracle, another reminder of the power of Jesus. It was a miracle intended to help Peter and the others to remember Jesus' divinity.

After they dragged the boat and net to shore, Jesus had breakfast ready for them. It was after this breakfast when Jesus pulled Peter aside to have a one-on-one conversation.

Before the crucifixion, Jesus had said to Peter,

> And I tell you that you are Peter, and on this rock I will build my church, and the gates of Hades will not overcome it. (Matt. 16:18)

Months earlier, Jesus had asked Peter, "Who do you say I am?" (Matt 16:15).

To which Peter had replied, "You are the Messiah, the Son of the living God" (Matt 16:16).

When Peter made this statement, he was right. Spiritually, Peter knew who and what Jesus was, but each time Peter was confronted with an opportunity to support this belief, in his human weakness, he reverted back to being Simon.

Now, sitting by the sea many days after the resurrection, Jesus was trying to cement Peter's new identity as *the Rock* and not Simon.

Two more times Jesus asks Peter, "Do you love me more than these?" Each time, Jesus was pressing Peter to fully commit. Jesus knew in a few days he was going to ascend into heaven, but first, he had to convince Peter to be *the Rock* and not revert back to being Simon.

Jesus knew Peter was his man, but he needed just a little more coaxing. With this question about *loving him more than these*, Jesus was prodding Peter to think about his future. Would Peter go back to his life as a fisherman, or would he go on to become *the Rock* upon which Jesus would build his church?

This was an intense moment in Peter's life; he knew there was a perceived sense of safety in staying where he was comfortable. He could continue fishing and socializing with his friends, looking back on his time with Jesus as a pleasant memory.

But Peter also knew what Jesus was asking of him—to give all that up and believe in the mission of serving Jesus and humankind. Peter knew this decision would lead to uncomfortable moments if he was going to achieve what Jesus was asking of him.

Peter sat, silently tossing the alternatives around. Torn, he went back and forth in his mind about the decision. He had seen those who had attacked and threatened Jesus. He knew this would likely happen to him as well. He had a decision to make: *lead a mediocre, comfortable life with few challenges or surrender to Jesus' request and lead a great life filled with difficult times?*

Peter did finally surrender. And after firmly cementing Christianity in Judea, he would leave and go to Rome, the then center of Western civilization.

Rome was a place of difficulty for Peter. The ruling class was uncomfortable with this new way of life of following Jesus. As such, Peter had to deal with persecution and distrust. But it was in Rome where Peter would drop Jesus' pollen and help set off the great evangelistic expansion of the Christian way.

Despite the prevailing persecutions against Christians and the widespread distrust of many in the power of Christianity, Peter strengthened the Christian church while residing in Rome. He accomplished what Jesus saw in him; he became *the Rock.* In fact, Peter became the first head of the church in Rome—the first pope.

Peter, much like Jesus, faced a death sentence at the hands of the Roman authorities. Destined for crucifixion, he felt unworthy to die in the same manner as Jesus. Out of this deep reverence, he requested to be crucified upside-down. The Romans honored his wish, leading to his upside-down crucifixion and subsequent burial in Rome. Today, his remains are believed to rest where the Vatican stands. This claim was substantiated in 1968.[43]

Amazingly, the Roman leaders thought killing Peter would end the expansion of Christianity. Instead, as we know today, Christianity blossomed. Like Peter, many others in the early days of

Christianity would die because of their refusal to worship the Roman gods. The Romans didn't stamp out Christianity; instead, they gave people martyrs to encourage their faith in Jesus.

In AD 313, Emperor Constantine issued the Edict of Milan, which granted legal status to Christianity. Later in AD 323, Constantine accepted Jesus as his savior and made Christianity the state religion of the Roman Empire.[44]

John Becomes the "Son of Love"

The apostle John was the youngest of the apostles.[45] As we know, because of his and his brother's abrupt and brash natures, they were called the *Sons of Thunder*. John could be very self-centered. Earlier, when Jesus told the apostles about his cruel and impending death, instead of offering support, stunningly, John selfishly asked if he could sit at Jesus' right hand when he came into his kingdom.

John's mother, the original helicopter parent, pressed Jesus to make her sons second-in-charge, contributing to John's youthful sense of entitlement.

Earlier in their time together, Jesus and the Twelve looked to rest at a village in Samaria. The leaders of the village rejected the request because they heard the group was also heading to Jerusalem, a rival city. After they were rejected by the village leaders, in his brashness, John asked Jesus if he could destroy the village. Naturally, Jesus turned to him and rebuked him (Lk. 9:56).

Over time, Jesus chiseled John to not be so brusque. John matured and, by the late first century, became a sought-after source of inspiration and a respected spiritual advisor.

John developed a loyal following, and one person in particular, Polycarp, was a student of John's. Polycarp, an early Christian historian, went on to write about John, thankfully leaving us with an insider's view of one of the original Twelve.

Polycarp (AD 69–155) was a priest and a professor. After the death of his mentor, he undertook the research project of locating and interviewing individuals who had interacted with Jesus. Upon finding John in Ephesus, he collaborated with him and learned about Jesus directly from John.

Polycarp devoted his life to collecting scrolls and artifacts about Jesus' life, striving to ensure that Jesus' message was accurately conveyed for future generations.

Though not widely recognized, Polycarp, through his writings, provides us with amazing firsthand information about Jesus.

From AD 41 to 44, Christian persecution in Jerusalem was particularly severe, and the apostles began leaving Judea to preach and minister in other parts of the world. Tradition holds that John went to nearby Turkey and ministered near Ephesus. In AD 95, John died of natural causes, making him the only one of the Twelve to not die a martyr.

By the time John died, he was totally transformed. The once brash and abrupt apostle had become a messenger of love and had earned the name *the Son of Love*.

Jesus Ascends

Before Jesus ascended on the fortieth day after he rose, he made one last appearance. At this time, there were many loyal followers of Jesus.[46] Jesus made one last statement to them:

> Do not leave Jerusalem, but wait for the gift my Father promised, which you have heard me speak about. For John baptized with water, but in a few days you will be baptized with the Holy Spirit. (Acts 1:4–5)

The group asked Jesus, "Lord, are you at this time going to restore the Kingdom of Israel?"

But Jesus had bigger plans and told them,

> It is not for you to know the times or dates the Father has set by his own authority. But you will receive power when the Holy Spirit comes on you; and you will be my

witnesses in Jerusalem, and in all Judea and Samaria,
and to the ends of the earth. (Acts 1:7–8)

Their mission was not just to witness about Jesus in Jerusalem
and the surrounding area, but to spread the message throughout the
world. After saying this, Jesus rose up into the clouds.

Ten days later, the Holy Spirit descended on the group. That
day is now called the Day of the Pentecost. Fifty days had passed
between the resurrection and the arrival of the Holy Spirit. This day
marked the beginning of the Christian church's mission to the
world.

Things did not end well for either Caiaphas or Pilate. Both were
dismissed from their positions in AD 36, according to early Jewish
historian Josephus.[47] Not only had the brutal crucifixion of Jesus created uproar with the Jewish population, but the persistent corruption also created an unstable environment as well. Seeking to calm
the population, the Roman leadership deposed of both men.

Pilate was recalled to Rome to stand trial for his injustices by
the then-Roman emperor Tiberius. Interestingly, the complaints
about him that caused Rome to dismiss him also came from the Samaritans, the longtime archenemies of the people of Jerusalem.[48]

On his way from Jerusalem to Rome, Tiberius died. His replace-
ment, Caligula, just starting his rule, ignored his predecessor's com-
mands regarding Pilate.[49] After this event, not much is known about
what happened to Pilate.

In AD 66, the people of Jerusalem revolted. As was generally
the case when territories revolted, Rome led a ruthless attack to re-
take Jerusalem. The people of Jerusalem fought valiantly against the
powerful Roman army, and at times, it appeared they would prevail.

In AD 70, they dug a tunnel under the temple to the location
where the Romans were preparing to attack. They created a great
fire in the tunnel under the Roman army, killing many. But at the
same time, this weakened the walls surrounding the temple, most of
which crumbled.

After this, no longer protected by the walls and exposed to the sheer size of the Roman army, they were defeated. Many of the citizens of Jerusalem were slain, and blood ran in the streets. In a lust for violence and greed, the Roman soldiers entered the inner sanctum of the temple. The soldiers had hoped for a rich bounty of loot; instead, they were disappointed.

The gold in the temple had melted in the fire set by the defenders of Jerusalem. The Roman soldiers destroyed what remained of the temple to recover the melted gold. Today, all that remains of the temple is a retaining wall of the original foundation called the Wailing Wall.[50]

As was previously stated, Jesus had predicted this as he left the temple on Tuesday of his Holy Week. As they walked past the temple, he addressed those who were admiring its beauty:

> "Do you see all these things?" he asked. "Truly I tell you, not one stone here will be left on another; every one will be thrown down." (Matt. 24:2)

The New Temple

With the crucifixion and resurrection of Jesus, a new temple was born, though our faith that Jesus is our Savior we are part of this new temple. As the Apostle Paul proclaimed, "Do you not know that your body is a temple of the Holy Spirit within you?" (1 Cor. 6:19–20).

In this verse, the word "you" refers to both the individual and the collective body of Christians. We are all embodiments of God's temple. The Holy Spirit resides within each of us, guiding and inspiring and establishing a direct connection through Jesus to God. Because of this and our creation in the image of God, both our bodies and souls are part of the eternal temple.

Christianity Continues to Grow

The remaining apostles all did spread out and take the message of Jesus to the ends of the earth. Thomas went to India. Peter went to Rome. Paul, a later convert, was most prolific and spread the word throughout the Mediterranean area.

Today, despite mainstream media news reports of a decline in the number of Jesus followers, the people who believe and have faith in the Easter story continues to grow worldwide. It is estimated by 2050, those believing will grow from two billion to three billion.[51]

Today, Jesus' followers experience Jesus through answers to prayers, which create an unexplainable sense of joy. He can be found today in quiet meditation or through an anxious plea for help. Jesus is seen through the eyes of mothers at the birth of a child. Jesus is felt by those who receive miracles, both small and big.

Even in creation, we can see Jesus' handiwork. While in theological school, a fellow student told us about a time when he was standing in a dreary parking lot with drug needles and empty liquor bottles strewn throughout the area. He looked up into the sky on a clear night with the brightness of stars twinkling, and this vision of creation overwhelmed him. In this moment, he felt Jesus and surrendered to him.

Similarly, the great twentieth-century Christian author C. S. Lewis was sitting alone in a room at Oxford University in 1929. For years, he had tried to logically avoid accepting Jesus, but on this night, all his arguments were too weak and feeble. Finally, he gave in and admitted to himself *God is God*, and he accepted Jesus. He described his surrendering to Jesus this way: "I gave in and prayed: perhaps that night I was the most dejected and reluctant convert in all of England."[52]

Army medics will tell you of stories of dying soldiers seeing Jesus as they died. And certainly, there are many cases of those who died but revived, describing their experience with Jesus. And he is with us today!

Jesus triumphantly rose that wonderful Easter morning, and his presence resonates among us today. Through his monumental victory on the cross, he unlocked the gates of redemption and salvation, offering every soul a chance to be saved by faith.

On bended knees, let us all rejoice, and have a good morning! Amen!

ENDNOTES

[1] Savada, Jack, "Meet Caiaphas: The High Priest of the Jerusalem Temple." https://www.learnreligions.com/caiaphas-high-priest-of-the-jerusalem-temple-701058, March 4th, 2021.

[2] Metzger, Bruce M.; Coogan, Michael, eds. (1993). *Oxford Companion to the Bible*. Oxford, England: Oxford University Press. p. 97. ISBN 978-0195046458.

[3] Perowne (2003). *Herod the Great*. pp. 92–93. ISBN 0-7509-3273-2.

[4] "The Roman Empire," https://www.pbs.org/empires/romans/empire/

[5] https://www.newscientist.com/article/dn1844-gruesome-death-for-brutal-biblical-ruler/

[6] https://www.ccel.org/j/josephus/works/ant-17.htm

[7] https://www.biblecharts.org/biblelandnotes/Distances%20From%20Jerusalem.pdf

[8] "Gate of Mercy - Shaar HaRachamim". Israel Forever Foundation. Retrieved 2021-12-27.

[9] Nylund, Jan, Court of the Gentiles. *Lexham Bible Dictionary*, Lexham Press. January 2016.

[10] Ibid

[11] https://acts242study.com/the-dividing-wall/

[12] Fredricksen, Paula; Temple Culture-Why the Temple Symbolized the Nation of Israel and Collaboration with the Romans

[13] https://truthbook.com/jesus/how-the-temple-was-profaned/

[14] https://www.dawsoncreekmirror.ca/opinion/sacrificial-lambs-and-swaddling-cloths-3506428

[15] https://truthbook.com/jesus/how-the-temple-was-profaned/

[16] https://www.bible.ca/coins/bible-coins-Jesus-used-in-the-New-Testament.htm

[17] "Shiloh, Israel's Capital for 400 Years, Being Uncovered," Gil Ronen, July 28, 2010, *The Jerusalem Post.*

[18] https://www.britannica.com/topic/Temple-of-Jerusalem

[19] Ibid

[20] https://www.britannica.com/topic/high-priest

[21] Nappa, Mike. Christianity.com, May 15th, 2019

[22] Ibid

[23] Ibid

[24] Bolinger, Hope. Crosswalk.com, Oct. 10th, 2019.

[25] Morris, "The Measure of Civilization" Date 2013.

[26] "Third Punic War," https://www.britannica.com/event/Third-Punic-War

[27] Center for Disease Control, https://www.cdc.gov/leprosy/index.html

[28] https://thewordmadefresh.org/sermons/faces-and-places-around-the-cross-si-mon-of-cyrene/

[29] https://www.britannica.com/biography/Moses-Hebrew-prophet

[30] https://www.worldhistory.org/article/1363/passover-in-the-hebrew-bible/

[31] https://www.agapebiblestudy.com/charts/jewishtimedivision.htm

[32]https://plantura.garden/uk/trees-shrubs/olive-tree/olive-tree-overview.

[33] https://www.stpeter-gallicantu.org/A-holy-place-in-Jerusalem-44.html?lang=en

[34] https://www.seetheholyland.net/tag/house-of-caiaphas/

[35] Marilyn Sams. "Antonia: The Fortress Jerusalem Forgot," Popular Archaeology, Summer 2022, 12/17/2015. https://popular-archaeology.com/article/antonia-the-fortress-jerusalem-forgot/

[36] https://christiananswers.net/q-abr/abr-a013.html

[37] https://www.catholiceducation.org/en/controversy/common-misconceptions/taking-the-measure-of-relics-of-the-true-cross.html

[38] Ibid

[39] Bryant, T.A., ed. (1982). *Today's Dictionary of the Bible.* Minneapolis: Bethany House. p. 580. ISBN 9780871235695. LCCN 82012980. OCLC 8669410.

[40] Reid, George (1913). "Acta Pilati". In Herbermann, Charles (ed.). *Catholic Encyclopedia*. New York: Robert Appleton Company.

[41] Wilhelm Schneemelcher, R. McLachlan Wilson (December 1, 1990) New Testament Apocrypha, Vol. 1 ISBN 0-66422721-X pp. 501–02

[42] https://jesusmemoirs.wordpress.com/2016/04/20/the-apostle-thomas-as-the-beloved-disciple/

[43] Guarducci, Margherita. "The Tomb of St. Peter." Hawthorn Books. Archived from the original on 29 April 2009. Retrieved 27 May 2009.

[44] https://www.pbs.org/empires/romans/empire/christians.html

[45] https://aleteia.org/2023/05/03/why-is-st-john-the-apostle-always-depicted-without-a-beard/

[46] https://christianityfaq.com/how-many-followers-did-jesus-christ-have/

[47] https://www.jewishvirtuallibrary.org/caiaphas-joseph

[48] https://www.internationalstandardbible.com/P/pilate-pontius.html

[49] https://www.internationalstandardbible.com/P/pilate-pontius.html

[50] https://www.britannica.com/topic/Temple-of-Jerusalem

[51] https://www.pewresearch.org/religion/2015/04/02/religious-projections-2010-2050/

[52] https://www.ncregister.com/blog/how-did-c-s-lewis-convert

Made in the USA
Middletown, DE
23 February 2024